The Yoga Sutras of Patañjali

Letter from the General Editor

The Library of Arabic Literature makes available Arabic editions and English translations of significant works of Arabic literature, with an emphasis on the seventh to nineteenth centuries. The Library of Arabic Literature thus includes texts from the pre-Islamic era to the cusp of the modern period, and encompasses a wide range of genres, including poetry, poetics, fiction, religion, philosophy, law, science, travel writing, history, and historiography.

Books in the series are edited and translated by internationally recognized scholars. They are published in parallel-text and English-only editions in both print and electronic formats. PDFs of Arabic editions are available for free download. The Library of Arabic Literature also publishes distinct scholarly editions with critical apparatus and a separate Arabic-only series aimed at young readers.

The Library encourages scholars to produce authoritative Arabic editions, accompanied by modern, lucid English translations, with the ultimate goal of introducing Arabic's rich literary heritage to a general audience of readers as well as to scholars and students.

The publications of the Library of Arabic Literature are generously supported by Tamkeen under the NYU Abu Dhabi Research Institute Award G1003 and are published by NYU Press.

Philip F. Kennedy
General Editor, Library of Arabic Literature

About this Paperback

This paperback edition differs in a few respects from its dual-language hardcover predecessor. Because of the compact trim size the pagination has changed. Material that referred to the Arabic edition has been updated to reflect the English-only format, and other material has been corrected and updated where appropriate. For information about the Arabic edition on which this English translation is based and about how the LAL Arabic text was established, readers are referred to the hardcover.

The Yoga Sutras of Patañjali

by

Abū Rayḥān al-Bīrūnī

translated by
Mario Kozah

foreword by
David Gordon White

volume editors
Kevin van Bladel
Shawkat M. Toorawa

NEW YORK UNIVERSITY PRESS
New York

NEW YORK UNIVERSITY PRESS
New York

Library of Congress Cataloging-in-Publication Data

Names: Bīrūnī, Muḥammad ibn Aḥmad, 973?–1048, author. | Kozah, Mario, 1976– translator. | White, David Gordon, writer of foreword.
Title: The yoga sutras of Patañjali / Abū Rayḥān al-Bīrūnī ; translated by Mario Kozah ; foreword by David Gordon White.
Other titles: Kitāb Bātanjal al-Hindī fī al-khalāṣ min al-irtibāk. English
Description: New York : New York University Press, 2022. | Includes bibliographical references and index. | Summary: "The Yoga Sutras of Patañjali is the foundational text of yoga philosophy, used by millions of yoga practitioners and students worldwide. This book is a new rendering into English of the Arabic translation and commentary of this text by the brilliant eleventh-century polymath al-Bīrūnī"— Provided by publisher.
Identifiers: LCCN 2021054336 | ISBN 9781479813216 (paperback) | ISBN 9781479813186 (ebook) | ISBN 9781479813209 (ebook)
Subjects: LCSH: Patañjali. Yogasūtra—Adaptations—History and criticism. | Yoga. | Sufism—Relations—Hinduism.
Classification: LCC B132.Y6 P278611349 2022 | DDC 181/.452—dc23/eng/20211116
LC record available at https://lccn.loc.gov/2021054336

Series design and composition by Nicole Hayward
Typeset in Adobe Text

Manufactured in the United States of America

10 9 8 7 6 5 4 3 2 1

For my wife, Rachelle

ܫܘܒܚܐ ܕܟܬܒܐ

ܠܐܢܬܬܝ ܪܚܝܠ

ܘܪܚܝܠ ܫܦܝܪܐ ܗܘܬ ܒܚܙܘܗ̇

ܘܝܐܐ ܡܘܒܠܠܗ̇

ܫܝܬ

ܟܛ

⁘

Contents

Foreword

DAVID GORDON WHITE

One of "the greatest scientific minds between antiquity and the Renaissance,"[1] Abū Rayḥān al-Bīrūnī's (362–440/973–1048) range of interests was phenomenal, extending from astronomy and mathematics to geography, physics, geology, psychology, mineralogy, pharmacology, and comparative religion. While it was his expertise in the first of these areas that likely brought him into the employ of some of the most glittering courts of his day—as an astronomer-astrologer (*munajjim*)[2]—it was his interest in comparative religion that was the driving force behind his extensive writings on Hindu religion and philosophy, including his translation of the *Yoga Sutras*. A native of the city-state of Khwārazm (modern-day Turkmenistan and Uzbekistan), he had been serving in the court of the Khwārazm-Shāhs at Gurganj (modern-day Urgench) when the principality was invaded and annexed by the armies of the powerful Ghaznavid emperor Maḥmūd in the year 1017 AD.[3] Whereas Edward Sachau (the translator of al-Bīrūnī's massive tome on India, about which more shortly) has asserted that al-Bīrūnī was taken to Maḥmūd's capital of Ghazna (modern-day eastern Afghanistan) as a hostage, others, including the translator of the present splendid volume, have viewed his transfer there as a more opportunistic move, a courtier's adaptation to the political winds of change. Regardless of the conditions of his "involuntary immigration," al-Bīrūnī would spend many if not most of the following thirteen years in the northwest of the Indian subcontinent, mainly in the Punjab.[4] It is likely that his Indian sojourns coincided with Maḥmūd's imperialistic project of empire-building, for the latter's annual campaigns in the subcontinent only ended with his death in 1030, which was also the year in which al-Bīrūnī "seem[ed] to have forgotten about India" after having penned some twenty volumes on the subject of the country, its traditions, and its inhabitants.[5] It was in the middle of that highly productive period, in the late 1020s, that he composed his *Kitāb Bātanjali al-Hindī*, an Arabic-language translation of and commentary on the *Yoga Sutras*.

A polyglot scholar, al-Bīrūnī would have had sufficient time during the decade between his arrival in the Ghaznavid court and the composition of his *Kitāb Bātanjali* to study Hindu culture first-hand, and to gain some level of proficiency in Sanskrit, the language of the *Yoga Sutras* and Hindu scriptural and scientific literature. He addresses the difficulty of mastering that language in the opening pages of his massive work *Hind* ("India"),[6] composed in 1030, in which he notes its intrinsic complexity, his difficulty in finding Hindu scholars capable of aiding him in his translations, and the necessity of understanding the contexts, literary and cultural, in which the meanings of its terms were embedded.[7] Collaborating with traditional Sanskrit scholars (*paṇḍit*s) and scriptural exegetes (*śāstrī*s) in both the Punjab and Ghazna itself, his apprenticeship in the language likely anticipated that of the European Orientalists of the late eighteenth and nineteenth centuries. Like them, he originally would have been entirely dependent upon these scholars as they provided him with running translations of the works in which he was interested, via Persian or a western Punjabi vernacular current at the time. Then, over the years, he became sufficiently familiar with the Sanskrit of his sources to translate them into Arabic with less outside assistance,[8] in some cases improving on the original Sanskrit in the manuscripts concerning the topic on which he was a world authority: astronomy.[9] Furthermore, in the *Hind* he speaks of translations *into Sanskrit* of works by Euclid and Ptolemy, composed by none other than himself.[10]

Throughout the same period, al-Bīrūnī was also increasing his cultural literacy with respect to the ways of the Hindus, eventually mastering several of their scientific disciplines in ways unprecedented by any foreign scholar, and unequalled by any for several centuries after him. An idea of his learning curve may be gained by juxtaposing statements made in his preface to the *Kitāb Bātanjali* and his preface to the *Hind*. In the earlier *Kitāb Bātanjali*, he speaks of the books he had previously translated on arithmetic and astronomy, and of his recently gained access to works on philosophy, which, when they had been read out to him "letter by letter," had permitted him to understand and communicate their content in the form of his own translation.[11] Some five years later, he concludes his preface to the *Hind* with an observation that attests to the pivotal role that the *Kitāb Bātanjali* translation had played in his study of Hinduism "on the ground":

> I have already translated two books into Arabic, one about the *origines* and a description of all created beings, called *Sâmkhya*, and another about the emancipation of the soul from the fetters of the body, called *Patañjali*. These two books contain most of the elements of the belief of the Hindus, but not all the single rules derived therefrom. I hope that the present book will enable the reader to dispense with these two earlier ones, and with other books of the same kind . . .[12]

Our sole copy of al-Bīrūnī's *Kitāb Bātanjali* has come down to us in corrupted form on the margins of the late fourteenth-century manuscript of an unrelated text. That it was discovered in an archive in Istanbul is significant inasmuch as it attests to the fact that by the beginning of the second millennium, the *Yoga Sutras* had become something of a global phenomenon.[13] Less than a century earlier, at the eastern extremity of the Muslim world, a work written in Old Javanese titled *Dharma Pātañjala* ("Sacred Teaching of Patañjali") contained a paraphrase of the *Yoga Sutras* similar to al-Bīrūnī's, this time embedded in an exposition of a Śaiva system of knowledge.[14] Like al-Bīrūnī's *Kitāb Bātanjali* but unlike Patañjali's original *Yoga Sutras*, the *Dharma Pātañjala* was presented as a dialogue.

Back in India, al-Bīrūnī's translation appeared at a time when that work and the philosophical school it represented were at their peak of their popularity, a situation that may explain why he identified the *Yoga Sutras* as an essential guide to Hindu philosophy. Such may well have been the case in the tenth and eleventh centuries, when the two most important commentaries on Patañjali's work, Vacaspati Miśra's *Tattvavaiśāradī* ("Expert Guide to the True Principles") and Bhoja's *Rājamārtaṇḍavṛtti* ("Royal Sun Commentary") were compiled. These two commentaries have the distinction of taking the *Yoga Sutras*' teachings at face value, and of elucidating them rather than arguing against them, as was the case with nearly all later pre-twentieth-century commentaries. This strange state of affairs may be explained on the basis of changes in the Hindu philosophical landscape taking place in al-Bīrūnī's time, and which likely influenced his own interpretation in significant ways.

Another commentary, the *Pātañjalayogaśāstrabhāṣyavivaraṇa* ("Exposition of the Commentary on Patañjali's Yoga Teaching") exemplifies this shift, inasmuch as it takes the position that the *puruṣa*s, the individual "persons" of the *Yoga Sutras,* are not multiple but singular, with Puruṣa denoting the Supreme Being who created the universe, who dwells in everything, and who is the object of Hindu devotion. This non-dualist position, which runs counter to the *Yoga Sutras*' Sāmkhya-based dualism, is of a piece with the tenets of the Advaita Vedānta school, whose greatest champion Śaṅkarācārya lived and taught in the ninth century. It is for this reason that some scholars have suggested that Śaṅkarācārya was himself the author of the "Exposition."[15] Regardless of this question of authorship, what can be said is that the fortunes of the Advaita Vedānta school would rise in inverse proportion to the diminishing popularity of the Yoga school, the tenets of whose foundational *Yoga Sutras* would come to be consistently read—or, more properly speaking, undermined—from a distorting Advaita Vedānta perspective. By the twelfth century, Advaita Vedānta had so monopolized the field of Hindu philosophy that no subsequent *Yoga Sutras* commentary respected the original text's foundational metaphysical positions. By the same token, commentaries on the *Yoga Sutras*, already relatively few and far between, became increasingly rare in the centuries that followed, prior to the work's meteoric return to prominence in the late twentieth century.

But in al-Bīrūnī's time, the *Yoga Sutras* were still very much in vogue in India, with important commentaries on and adaptations of the work being compiled by figures like the great Śrīvaiṣṇava theologian Rāmānuja and the twelfth-century Jain philosopher Hemacandra. However, these too were circumspect in their treatment of yoga philosophy, taking issue with Patañjali on a number of points. While the Hindu Rāmānuja was not a proponent of Advaita Vedānta philosophy,[16] many of the positions he took were grounded in the same Hindu doctrines of faith as those of the Advaitins, doctrines that were championed in the massive medieval compendia of Hindu thought and practice that were the Purāṇas ("Antiquarian Books"). Teachings on yoga from the same Purāṇas were likely in the minds of al-Bīrūnī's *paṇḍit*s, and it is here that certain elements of his treatment of the *Yoga Sutras* may be viewed as indicative of the general state of scripture-based religious knowledge in early eleventh-century India.

Most significant in this regard is al-Bīrūnī's account of the final goal of yoga, as disclosed in both the *Kitāb Bātanjali* and the *Hind*. As the final verse of Patañjali's Sanskrit original explains, the practice of yogic meditation culminates in the isolation (*kaivalyam*) of the individual *puruṣa* from materiality (*prakṛti*), with "the energy of pure consciousness [being] grounded in its own inherent form."[17] In his translation, al-Bīrūnī translates *kaivalyam* as "liberation" (*khalāṣ*) further implying that this was also linked to "unification" (*ittiḥād*).[18] The first seven chapters of his *Hind*—which, written immediately after the *Kitāb Bātanjali*, contain further reflections on the philosophy of the *Yoga Sutras*[19]—identify liberation "according to the Hindus" as "union with God."[20] Taken together, these data support the conclusion that "al-Bīrūnī's Arabic version characteristically speaks of the goal of yoga as 'liberation and union with God'."[21] While this significant diversion from the letter and spirit of Patañjali's work may simply be a reflection of the limits of translation across the barriers of language and culture,[22] it also likely sheds light on the religious and philosophical orientations of certain of the *paṇḍits* with whom al-Bīrūnī collaborated in crafting his translation. Non-dualist philosophy being most congenial to the spirit of Hindu devotion (*bhakti*), the goal of all practice was fast becoming the realization that all was one and internal to God, with knowledge of this non-difference being sufficient to the realization of that underlying identity. This, union with God, was tantamount to salvation, to liberation from suffering existence (*mokṣa*).

Another possible clue to the state of the Yoga system at the time is a name embedded in al-Bīrūnī's "Prologue" to the *Kitāb Bātanjali*,[23] which contains a "benediction" not found in any extant Sanskrit-language work of the period. That benediction concludes with the clause "the summary exposition I wish to make in the style of Hiraṇyagarbha."[24] Who was Hiraṇyagarbha? Literally the "Golden Embryo," the name first and foremost refers to Brahmā, the divine demiurge of puranic mythology and mythic father of a number of "mind-born" sons expert in yoga. The earliest attestation of this epithet is found in India's great epic, the *Mahābhārata*,[25] which also identifies him as the divine revealer of the Yoga system.[26] The Purāṇas, which immediately follow the *Mahābhārata* in the chronology of Hindu scripture, repeat and amplify this identification, naming Hiraṇyagarbha, and *not* Patañjali, as the founder of the Yoga system. Although this possibility is addressed and immediately rejected by the aforementioned Vacaspati Miśra in his commentary to the *Yoga Sutras*' opening verse,[27] no other commentator prior to or contemporary with al-Bīrūnī mentions this figure. However, several Purāṇas known to both him and many later commentators ascribe this honor to Hiraṇyagarbha,[28] and a lost work titled *Hiraṇyagarbhayogaśāstra* ("Hiraṇyagarbha's Yoga Teaching") is quoted in many of these sources. Another work attributed to the same figure and preserved in a redacted form within a Vaiṣṇava scripture is the *Hiraṇyagarbha Saṃhitā* ("Hiraṇyagarbha's Collection").[29] These data notwithstanding, Hiraṇyagarbha's Yoga system was, like Hiraṇyagarbha himself, mythical.

When in the early nineteenth century the British Orientalists first began to investigate yoga philosophy and the *Yoga Sutras*, they generally turned to the *paṇḍit*s for guidance. Almost invariably, these perennial custodians of Hindu tradition cited Puranic lore, rather than Patañjali's treatise, as the essence of yoga, even as they attributed that Puranic lore to Patañjali himself![30] This state of affairs has continued down to the present day among India's yoga gurus, whose accounts of the *Yoga Sutras* are generally non-dualist and theistic, in accordance with Puranic accounts of the Yoga system. Outstanding scholar that he was, al-Bīrūnī cast a wide net in the preparation of his Arabic version of the *Yoga Sutras*, complementing his own philological prowess and philosophical expertise with the "local knowledge" of the yoga aficionados he consulted. The fact that he refers in his prologue to Hiraṇyagarbha is an indication that the yogic knowledge of certain of those collaborators was faith-based rather than grounded in a tradition of commentarial exegesis.

David Gordon White
University of California, Santa Barbara

Notes to the Foreword

1 S. Frederick Starr, "Rediscovering Central Asia," *Wilson Quarterly 33, no. 6* (Summer 2009): 33.

2 Edward C. Sachau, *Alberuni's India: An Account of the Religion, Philosophy, Literature, Geography, Chronology, Astronomy, Customs, Laws, and Astrology of India about 1030* (London: Kegan Paul, Trench, Trübner, 1910; Delhi: Munshiram Manoharlal, 1983), 1: ix.

3 C. E. Bosworth, "The Political and Dynastic History of the Iranian World (A.D. 1000–1217)," in J. A. Boyle, ed., *The Cambridge History of Iran*, vol. 5, *The Seljuq and Mongol Periods* (Cambridge: Cambridge University Press, 2007), 8.

4 Sachau, 1: ix.

5 Sachau, 1: xvi, xxvii.

6 The full Arabic title reads: *Kitāb Taḥqīq mā li-l-Hind min maqūlah maqbūlah fī-l-ʿaql aw mardhūlah.*

7 Sachau, 1: 17, 24.

8 Suniti Kumar Chatterji, "Al-Bīrūnī and Sanskrit," in *Al-Bīrūnī Commemoration Volume, A.H. 362–A.H. 1362* (Calcutta: Iran Society, 1951), 86–87.

9 Sachau, 1: xxxvii.

10 Sachau, 1: 137.

11 Abū Rayḥān al-Bīrūnī, *The Yoga Sutras of Patañjali*, edited and translated by Mario Kozah (New York: New York University Press, 2020), xvi, §0.3.

12 Sachau, 1: 8.

13 The French Islamicist Louis Massignon documents his discovery of the manuscript in his *Essai sur les origines du lexique technique de la mystique musulmane* (Paris: Paul Guethner, 1922), 79 n. 1.

14 Andrea Acri, "Dharma Pātañjala, A Śaiva Scripture from Ancient Java: Studied in the Light of Related Old Javanese and Sanskrit Texts," PhD dissertation, Leiden University (2011), 477–550.

15 Trevor Leggett, *The Complete Commentary by Śaṅkara on the Yoga Sūtras: A Full Translation of the Newly Discovered Text* (London: Kegan Paul International, 1990), 7–8, 18, 40–41, 107–34. Cf. Gerald James Larson and Ram Shankar Bhattacharya, eds., *Yoga: India's Philosophy of Meditation* (Delhi: Motilal Banarsidass, 2008), 239–40.

16 Rāmānuja's philosophical school was called Viśiṣṭādvaita ("Qualified Non-Dualism"), which differed from the "pure" non-dualism of Advaita Vedānta on the question of the existence of individual persons independent of a god with personal qualities, such as Viṣṇu.

17 *Yoga Sūtra 4.34: kaivalyam svarūpapratiṣṭhā . . . citiśaktir . . .*

18 al-Bīrūnī, *The Yoga Sutras of Patañjali*, §78.2–78.3, which ends with: "This concludes the fourth chapter on the subject of liberation and unification . . ."

19 al-Bīrūnī, *The Yoga Sutras of Patañjali*, xxi.

20 Sachau, 1: 81.

21 Tuvia Gelblum, "AL-BĪRŪNĪ, 'Book of Patañjali'," in Larson and Bhattacharya, 262. The Indonesian *Dharma Pātañjala* also identified the goal of practice as "union" with God: Acri, 495.

22 al-Bīrūnī, *The Yoga Sutras of Patañjali*, xxi.

23 al-Bīrūnī, *The Yoga Sutras of Patañjali*, §0.1–0.6.

24 al-Bīrūnī, *The Yoga Sutras of Patañjali*, §0.6.

25 *Mahābhārata* 12.202.33; 12.326.4.

26 *Mahābhārata* 12.337.60. Cf. 12.326.65; 12.330.31.

27 James Haughton Woods, *The Yoga-System of Patañjali* (Cambridge, MA: Harvard University Press 1914), 5.

28 Sachau, 1: 130–31; Jan Gonda, "Remarks on al-Bīrūnī's Quotations from Sanskrit Texts," in *Al-Bīrūnī Commemoration Volume*, 111.

29 Larson and Bhattacharya, 143; Ram Shankar Bhattacharya, *An Introduction to the Yogasutra* (Delhi: Bharatiya Vidya Prakashana, 1985), 16–19, 171–73.

30 David Gordon White, *The Yoga Sutra of Patañjali: A Biography* (Princeton, NJ: Princeton University Press, 2013), 45–48, 99.

Acknowledgments

I would like to thank the LAL executive board, Philip Kennedy, James Montgomery, and Shawkat Toorawa, for adopting this book project, and especially Shawkat Toorawa for his indefatigable energy, thoroughness, and exactitude while reviewing my manuscript. It was a privilege, pleasure, and education working with him. I am grateful to the LAL team, Chip Rossetti and Lucie Taylor, for safely steering me through the many stages of the rigorous publication process, which is truly unique and the most professional I have ever experienced. I thank the cohort of anonymous reviewers commissioned by LAL to comment on my work, who helped me iron out the inconsistencies and challenged me to reconsider many points I had taken for granted. I would also like to thank the cartographer, Martin Grosch, the copy editor, Keith Miller, and the digital production manager, Stuart Brown, for their useful input. Without the generosity and expeditious assistance of Zisan Furat, for which I am grateful, I would not have had access to a digital copy of the only known manuscript of this text.

My sincere gratitude to Nadia Maria El Cheikh, who back in 2003 hosted and chaired my first talk on al-Bīrūnī's psychology at the American University of Beirut (AUB) and has encouraged me to continue my research in this field ever since. A special thanks to Abdulrahim Abu-Husayn, whose wise counsel, contagious humor, and sincere friendship have been a vital lifeline through good times and bad. Heartfelt thanks to my inimitable Cambridge professor, AUB colleague, and academic guru Tarif Khalidi (TK), who took it upon himself, despite his many projects, to carefully comb through my translation and gild it with masterful touches. He urged me to pursue this project at its outset, describing an early draft as "a very impressive translation indeed. My only complaint is your utter contempt for punctuation!" I am also grateful to the indomitable David Wilmsen, head of the Department of Arabic and Translation Studies at the American University of Sharjah, who, only by way of encouragement I am sure, referred to an initial draft translation as "masterful." I am deeply indebted to Nader El-Bizri, old Cantabrigian friend and esteemed colleague, for many an inspiring conversation on Islamic science and philosophy over the years.

Thanks are due to my dear family friend Joseph Moufarrege, who never failed to ask me about the progress of this book project whenever we met for a drink or lunch. I wish to express deep gratitude to my dearest brother John-Paul for many a long conversation on topics related to psychology and philosophy, which often helped me sharpen my focus and think more deeply. Last but not least, I am forever indebted to my loves Rachelle, Karl, and Kristina for their affection, support, and, above all, incredible patience.

Introduction

Life and Times of al-Bīrūnī

Abū Rayḥān Muḥammad ibn Aḥmad al-Bīrūnī (d. ca. 440/1048) was one of the most famous scientists and polymaths in the history of Islamic civilization. His works rival those of illustrious contemporaries such as Ibn Sīnā in their depth and sophistication, but there has been little scholarly writing about him in the West relative to his importance. He was born in 362/973, probably in Kāth, which at that time was the capital of the city-state of Khwārazm, located in the Transoxania region of Central Asia,[1] an area witness to long years of direct and indirect cultural and linguistic influence by Persia, India, and even China. Thus, although al-Bīrūnī's native language was Khwārazmian, he was from the outset exposed to a spectrum of influences that shaped his lifelong passion for the close study of other civilizations and religions.

From 408/1017 till his death in ca. 440/1048, al-Bīrūnī found himself mostly in Ghazna (in modern-day Afghanistan), then the capital of the Ghaznavid Empire, in the courts and under the patronage of three Ghaznavid sultans, Maḥmūd (r. 408–21/1017–30), Masʿūd (r. 422–32/1031–41), and Mawdūd (r. 432–39/1041–48), and under their auspices he produced his greatest works. Under Maḥmūd he wrote his magnum opus on India, the *India* (ca. 421/1030);[2] under Maḥmūd's son and successor, Masʿūd ibn Maḥmūd, he wrote his landmark astronomical work, *Masʿūd's Canonical Rules on the Shape of the Universe and the Stars* (ca. 426/1035).[3]

Al-Bīrūnī's Philosophical and Intellectual Milieu

By the tenth century, Transoxania had produced some of the most remarkable figures in the intellectual history of Islam and in the fields of mathematics, hadith, *kalām*, and philosophy. Muḥammad ibn Mūsā al-Khwārazmī (d. ca. 232/847) is often considered to be the inventor of algebra, although he in fact developed this and other mathematical operations based on older Indian and Greek sources, which he was most likely first exposed to in Khwārazm. Shortly afterward, Muḥammad ibn Ismāʿīl al-Bukhārī (d. 256/870) compiled what is considered the preeminent hadith collection, the *Ṣaḥīḥ Bukhārī*. No less importantly, Abū Manṣūr Muḥammad al-Māturīdī (d. ca. 333/944), a famous theologian and a scholar of Islamic jurisprudence and Qurʾanic exegesis, founded one of the two foremost schools of Sunni theology, *kalām*, and was renowned as a pioneer in Islamic jurisprudence. Finally, two of the most prominent founding figures of the Arabic philosophical tradition, Abū Naṣr Muḥammad al-Fārābī (d. 339/950) and Abū ʿAlī al-Ḥusayn ibn Sīnā (d. 428/1037), also hail from this region of Central Asia. Al-Fārābī was a renowned Muslim scientist and philosopher, as well as an accomplished cosmologist, logician, and musician. Through his treatises, he became known among medieval Muslim intellectuals as "the Second Teacher"—that is, the successor to "the First Teacher," Aristotle. Al-Bīrūnī's contemporary Ibn Sīnā is considered the most famous and influential polymath of this Islamic golden age.

This is the intellectual milieu in which al-Bīrūnī was born and educated, and where he spent the first twenty-two years of his life, from 362/973 to 385/995, under the rule of the Āl-i ʿIrāq Khwārazmshāhs. Little biographical information can be verified from this early period of al-Bīrūnī's life; however, it would seem that he received his early education under a teacher by the name of Abū Naṣr Manṣūr ibn ʿAlī ibn ʿIrāq, whom he mentions in *The Vestiges of Bygone Eras* (*al-Āthār al-bāqiyah*),[4] one of his early works. In 385/995 al-Bīrūnī fled his home city when his patrons, the ruling dynasty of Āl-i ʿIrāq, were defeated at the hands of Āl-i Maʾmūn of Jurjāniyyah, an independent Iranian family. A period of wandering ensued, with al-Bīrūnī living at times in Khwārazm and at others in Jurjān, searching for patronage and permanent residence.

At some point during these difficult years (385–88/995–98), he initiated a correspondence with his rival Ibn Sīnā, who was probably living in Jurjāniyyah and in the service of the Āl-i Maʾmūn or the Maʾmūnids, from ca. 387/997 to 403/1012. It is unclear whether an actual meeting between the two took place, although such a hypothetical meeting would most probably have occurred in one of the Maʾmūnid courts. This correspondence, referred to as *Questions and Answers* (*al-Asʾilah wa-l-Ajwibah*),[5] is significant because it reveals the scientific and philosophical context in which al-Bīrūnī thought and worked. *Questions and Answers* consists of ten questions posed by al-Bīrūnī regarding the Arabic translation of Aristotle's *De Caelo et Mundo, The Heavens and the World* (*al-Samāʾ wa-l-ʿĀlam*), followed by eight additional questions that relate to a range of contentions within the Peripatetic (Ar. *mashshāʾī*) School of natural philosophy and that present a critical challenge to Ibn Sīnā, then the most eminent representative of this school. Ibn Sīnā answers each of the questions posed, with varying success. *Questions and Answers* exposes several of the most problematic scientific issues of the time and their metaphysical connotations, as well as the existence of an anti-Peripatetic current within contemporary Islamic intellectual circles.

The Peripatetic School dominated the philosophical tradition in Islamic civilization and colored much of the language of the great Muslim scientists, including al-Bīrūnī. *Questions and Answers* presents al-Bīrūnī's logical criticism of Peripatetic natural philosophy by questioning the basis of its reasoning and its science in a rigorous exchange of mutually comprehensible terminology. Whether al-Bīrūnī's logical criticism has a philosophical source derived, for example, from the Pythagorean-Hermetic heritage of antiquity or from his first encounters with Indian science, philosophy, and cosmological doctrines can only be gleaned by examining the contents of his many works and the nuances in the comparisons he makes.[6]

The importance of *Questions and Answers* lies not only in that it marks a key point in Islamic intellectual history, natural philosophy, and the sciences, but also in its foregrounding of a defining moment at the outset of al-Bīrūnī's career. By competing against the most famous intellectual rival of his time and choosing to differ on any number of a priori theories that form the basis of Aristotelian physics, al-Bīrūnī signaled his independence from the Peripatetic School and simultaneously established a tabula rasa from which to explore the empirical sciences and the development of ideas from new sources. The language used to express such ideas, though colored by Aristotle's dominant influence, belongs neither to al-Bīrūnī nor Ibn Sīnā, but rather derives from the lexicon of the Abbasid translators and the *falāsifah* written specifically to serve as a common language for philosophical dialectic. Interestingly, the intellectual rivalry between al-Bīrūnī and Ibn Sīnā is paralleled by the dynastic rivalries of the courts to which they belonged. Both the Ziyārids[7] and the Ghaznavids[8] in whose rulers al-Bīrūnī found patronage were the implacable rivals of the Buyids in whose courts Ibn Sīnā found favor.

In 388/998, most likely in Jurjān, al-Bīrūnī found in the Ziyārid Shams al-Maʿālī Qābūs ibn Wushmagīr (d. 403/1012 or 404/1013) his next significant patron. Under the apparently generous patronage of this fourth ruler of the Ziyārid dynasty of Ṭabaristān and Jurjān, al-Bīrūnī wrote *The Vestiges of Bygone Eras*, probably in 390/1000, dedicated to this new patron. It remains one of his greatest scholarly achievements, with its broad sweep of subject matter, especially its sections on astronomy, history, and religion. In 394/1004 al-Bīrūnī returned to Jurjāniyyah, the new capital of Khwārazm, to serve the Maʾmūnids, whose favor he had gained under the patronage of the Khwārazm-shāhs Abū l-Ḥasan ʿAlī (387–99 or

400/997–1008 or 1009) and Abū l-ʿAbbās al-Maʾmūn ibn Maʾmūn (d. 408/1017). During this period, al-Bīrūnī wrote a number of scientific works, including *Determining Location Coordinates to Correct Distances between Settlements* (*Kitāb Taḥdīd nihāyāt l-amākin li-taṣḥīḥ masāfāt l-masākin*), and also served the Maʾmūnid court in diplomatic and political posts. Following the betrayal and death of al-Maʾmūn in 408/1017, Maḥmūd of Ghazna (360–421/971–1030), the ruler of the Ghaznavid Empire, invaded Khwārazm under the pretext of avenging his brother-in-law's murder. With this annexation and the effective demise of the Maʾmūnids, al-Bīrūnī found himself (along with other prominent scholars, including Ibn Sīnā) adjusting to a new dynastic sphere of influence. While Ibn Sīnā and other scholars went west, al-Bīrūnī hesitated, and ultimately came under Maḥmūd's patronage. Whether this was a decision he took or that was taken for him remains unclear, as does the exact nature of his relationship with this new patron.

Kitāb Bātanjali al-Hindī

The present work, *Kitāb Bātanjali*, whose full title given in the manuscript is *Kitāb Bātanjali al-Hindī* (*The Book of Patañjali the Indian*), is al-Bīrūnī's Arabic translation of the Sanskrit *Yoga Sutras* of Patañjali. It was written in the late 410s/1020s, probably during al-Bīrūnī's travels in northeastern India. It is one of the most important surviving works of translation in the Islamic tradition of that century, revealing al-Bīrūnī's deep understanding of Yoga philosophy and the Sanskrit language, to which modern-day interpretations and studies still refer.

Kitāb Bātanjali was first discovered by Louis Massignon (1922), later described by Jakob Wilhelm Hauer (1930), and eventually published by Helmut Ritter with an introduction in German in 1956.[9] It is divided into four "sections" or "chapters" that correspond to the four chapters of the *Yoga Sutras* of Patañjali, but al-Bīrūnī also explicitly cites the explanations of an unnamed "commentator," argued in earlier studies to be Vyāsa, the great fifth-century commentator of the *Yoga Sutras*.[10] These studies also state that al-Bīrūnī not only draws on Vyāsa's *Yoga Bhāṣya*, but also on other unidentified commentators to illuminate Patañjali's thought.

In a pioneering study, "On Some Epistemological and Methodological Presuppositions of al-Bīrūnī," Franz Rosenthal argues that ideas found in the *Yoga Sutras* entered al-Bīrūnī's epistemological thinking:

> Normally, it would seem prudent for us to see in Bīrūnī more the reporter of Indian philosophical speculation than the follower of it. However, his receptive mind was often deeply impressed by the foreign ideas he studied, and they were incorporated into his thought patterns.[11]

As will be clear from the present volume, the particular psychological reading to be found in *Kitāb Bātanjali* represents an accurate reflection of Patañjali's Yoga, and to this extent clearly demonstrates that al-Bīrūnī had a profound and scientific comprehension of the ideas he was translating. *Kitāb Bātanjali* can no longer be thought of as a text that is a superficial reconstruction by its author of the original *Yoga Sutras* based on hearsay and oral reports, as some scholars still maintain.

The *Yoga Sutras* of Patañjali

The first systematization of Yoga took place in the *Yoga Sutras* attributed to Patañjali (possibly fourth or fifth century AD), and the philosophical implications of the *Sutras* were discussed soon after in a commentary traditionally attributed to Vyāsa. Historically, little if anything is known about Patañjali. It is reasonable to assume that, as head of a school of Yoga, Patañjali was an active preceptor or *guru* and, judging from the *Yoga Sutras*, a great authority on Yoga, whose approach was sympathetic toward philosophical inquiry and exposition.[12] It is also reasonable to suppose that Patañjali taught a community of disciples, *śisyas*, devoted to the study and practice of Yoga, who carried on the tradition of this philosophical school.[13]

Adopting a classical format written in *sutra* style, a style of writing often employed in the compositions of the so-called six orthodox systems of philosophy used within Hinduism, Patañjali composed the *Yoga Sutras* at a time of intense debate and philosophical speculation in India. As such, "he supplied Yoga with a reasonably homogenous framework that could stand up against the many rival traditions,"[14] including Nyāya, Vedānta, and Buddhism.

Just as Patañjali employed the *sutra* style to express Yoga within the framework of rival traditions, so too the terminology of contemporary Arabic philosophy is employed in *Kitāb Bātanjali* and the *Hind* to facilitate its accessibility within the framework of the dominant Peripatetic tradition to which Ibn Sīnā and the majority of Muslim thinkers of the time adhered.

The Structure and Contents of *Kitāb Bātanjali*

Kitāb Bātanjali follows a dialogic format that may have been inspired by Socratic treatises with which al-Bīrūnī was familiar. He was certainly familiar with a version of Plato's *Phaedo*, structured in a dialogic format, which he quotes extensively in the *Hind*.[15] Nevertheless, one cannot ignore the possibility of other influences on the structure of *Kitāb Bātanjali*, not least the question-and-answer format that exists in some of the earliest Muslim legal and theological texts, as well as in Arabic philosophical correspondences.[16] In addition, the pedagogical benefits of such a structure are reminiscent of the teacher-pupil dynamic in the Sufi oral and written traditions.

The use of the dialogic format highlights the priority given in Yoga to the guidance of a spiritual preceptor who has direct experience of the insights as well as the obstacles that may arise on the path to liberation. However, unlike Yoga—where the ideal is of a *guru* as "true teacher," having attained the ultimate realization informing all yogic endeavor—in *Kitāb Bātanjali* the teacher is the vehicle for the attainment of definitive proofs through the provision of which the disciple's "uncertainty and doubt" are dispelled (§1.1).

In addition to four chapters, *Kitāb Bātanjali* includes a tripartite prologue, the contents of which are primarily explanatory and pedagogical. It concludes with a brief epilogue containing a comparative dimension that anticipates the comprehensive depth and sophistication of the *Hind*, which was composed immediately after it. In the prologue, al-Bīrūnī describes the manner with which such texts were read to him word by word (lit. letter by letter; §0.3), and outlines the main topic of *Kitāb Bātanjali* as "liberation from afflictions."[17] This includes "propositions on transmigration and the sorrows of incarnation, as well as unification and generation not through the law of procreation" (§0.4). Al-Bīrūnī then highlights the significance and process of attaining liberation, which he describes as intimately bound with the state of the individual soul, summarized in terms of the "perfection of the soul through liberation from bondage, leading to the attainment of eternal bliss" (§0.6).

The questions and answers of the first chapter focus on the complex interaction of the soul with the body, in particular the means of achieving the concentration of the mind (referred to as "the heart" in the Arabic) that is a distinct concept in Yoga philosophy. To this end, three methods of spiritual ascesis are described: praxis (§6.2), intellectual dispassion (§6.2), and devotion (§11.2). These correspond to the three stages of Yoga elaborated in several Hindu works, including the *Bhagavad Gīta*: *karma yoga*, *bhakti yoga*, and *jñāna yoga*.[18] Reliance on these treatises in *Kitāb Bātanjali* may have been intended to enhance the principal aim of describing the theoretical and practical process of self-realization through concentration of the mind and liberation of the soul. After a subtle analysis outlining the five faculties of the soul, the dialogue shifts to a discussion of the three methods of spiritual ascesis.

The second chapter of *Kitāb Bātanjali* draws attention to the discipline required to achieve liberation. Al-Bīrūnī begins by describing the "afflictions that encumber the mind" (§26.1) and keep the soul in a state of entanglement. The five opinions listed in *Kitāb Bātanjali* reflect, although problematically and inconclusively, the five afflictions, *kleśas,* listed in *sutra* II.3.[19] The process of "liberation" is given an additional dimension in this second chapter of *Kitāb Bātanjali,* which involves the soul's gradual disentanglement from sense perception through a seven-stage progression that includes four outer and three inner stages of preparation (§39.2). Bodily withdrawal is now possible if one pursues the classical *yoga* system, often referred to as the eight-limbed path, *aṣṭāṅga yoga,* and referred to as such in *Kitāb Bātanjali* (§41.1). Exposition of this system spans the second and third sections of *Kitāb Bātanjali.* It constitutes the core of the argumentation that emphasizes the necessity of a pragmatic continuum enabling the transformation, rather than transcendence (as in the dualism of Sāṃkhya or the Peripatetic tradition), of the soul's consciousness and identity that alone can bring an end to its misidentification and ignorance.[20] Within these eight limbs, the empirical process is dealt with aspect by aspect in a manner that challenges a pure form of dualism with its bias for spiritual transcendence through separation from matter, rather than integration with it.[21] This is the culminating and longest stage of *Kitāb Bātanjali,* in which all actions, intentions, volitions, and thoughts are subjected to spiritual ascesis by which the soul is purified "through limbs that make the knower pure and holy" (§40.2).

After covering the remaining three limbs, the third chapter also focuses on recompense and the means by which requital is achieved. Thus, advancement through these limbs accomplishes spiritual purification and progress, and leads to the soul's self-realization beyond the individual, incarnate personality. *Kitāb Bātanjali* describes this progression in a manner that reflects the *Yoga Sutras* as a growing unification of mental consciousness that is the means to self-transcendence and spiritual liberation.[22] Thus, the third chapter concludes with the soul–body relationship being understood, first, not in terms of an utter distinctness between the two but as the removal of *karma* by means of recompense for past deeds and refraining from future ones. The one who arrives at the stage of liberation "has fulfilled his dues for past actions in his present form and withdrawn from acquiring any more *karma* for the future" (§47.2). Second, the soul–body relationship is understood in terms of a distinction in which the soul exists in a liberated state of union with the body (§47.2).

The fourth chapter treats the subject of liberation through unification. It evinces a perceptible development from the psychological to the intellectual: from a discussion of *nafs* in the preceding sections to a treatment of the role of *ʿaql* in the individual's existential endeavor toward liberation. This is achieved through a process of unification of the intellect and intellected with and within the prioritized role of the intellector.[23] Thus, it is implied that the intellector, *ʿāqil*, who achieves unification, *ittiḥād*, with the intellect and the intellected (§67.2) attains that which was initially postulated for the intellect—namely, knowing itself purely for itself (§70.1).

The Layers of Commentary in *Kitāb Bātanjali*

Since he never explicitly names him, it is uncertain whom al-Bīrūnī is referring to when he speaks of and quotes "the commentator" (§46.3). He clearly understands that "these texts come with commentaries" and "commentators," and he himself will blend the text of his "translation with the separate commentary" (§0.5) he has chosen to use, thus producing a text "interwoven" (§0.6) with that commentary, his own interpretations, and perhaps even insights from other commentaries he does not identify. He restructures the whole "discourse as a dialogue consisting of questions and answers," while removing "topics related to grammar and language" for the sake of conciseness, among other reasons (§0.5). In al-Bīrūnī's understanding, therefore, the text he is translating, restructuring, explaining, and editing is the work of the author whom he refers to explicitly by name as *Bātanjali*. In addition, he explicitly cites from an unnamed "commentator" of a "separate" commentary, informing the reader when this citation begins and when it ends (§46.3).

Al-Bīrūnī's text is, as a result, a multilayered Arabic translation and interpretation of the *Yoga Sutras* of Patañjali, the integrated commentary on it known as the bhāṣya (§0.5), and the comprehension of both by him, in addition to a "separate commentary" (§0.5) by an unnamed "commentator" whom he refers to whenever he cites it. Nevertheless, as the present translation and the table of correspondences[24] demonstrates, it is in fact possible to identify most of the content of each question and answer in *Kitāb Bātanjali* by tracking the individual *sutras* themselves without reference to any Sanskrit commentaries or even the so-called *Yoga Bhāṣya* part attributed to Vyāsa, all the while taking into consideration the scope for interpretation and explanation inherent in al-Bīrūnī's creative translation process. The basic subject matter of the questions and answers in the Arabic text run parallel to the *sutras* in almost exactly the same sequence as the standard Sanskrit version of Patañjali's *Yoga Sutras*.[25]

Al-Bīrūnī's translation represents a methodological project of interpreting and defining Hinduism along Islamic lines. His motives are conditioned in part by the challenge of contemporary philosophical debate within his cultural and intellectual sphere, which included such luminaries as Abū Bakr al-Rāzī (d. 313/925) and Ibn Sīnā. *Kitāb Bātanjali* is the product of the particular version of the Sanskrit text that al-Bīrūnī translated (itself a multivalent work combining text with commentary), and the oral and textual exegesis at his disposal in Ghazna. Given the lack of precise information relating to these layers and their identification, *Kitāb Bātanjali* ultimately eludes a full contextualization.

Al-Bīrūnī as a Commentator on Yoga

On a number of occasions in the prologue, al-Bīrūnī stresses the importance of the pursuit of knowledge, not least in the opening paragraph, where the attainment of learning necessitates a pedagogical obligation to impart it to others: "When these books were read out to me word by word and I had understood their content, my conscience made me want to share it with other interested readers" (§0.3). This sense of scholarly obligation was possibly inspired by the strong pedagogical current running through the *Yoga Sutras* itself, conveyed in the core structure of *Kitāb Bātanjali* through its dialogic format between Patañjali and a "renunciant" or *yogin*—a Yoga practitioner—reminiscent of the Ancient Greek and Syriac philosophical and spiritual dialogues, for example, John the Solitary's (ca. AD 390) *Dialogue on the Soul*[26] and Plato's *Phaedo*,[27] which al-Bīrūnī cites on a number of occasions in the *Hind*.

Earlier scholarship has tended to approach the work in a somewhat contradictory fashion, oscillating between al-Bīrūnī's eccentric, open-minded scholarship and a desire to cast him in the mold of Muslim cultural superiority. Such an approach overlooks the possibility that the internal philosophical dynamics of a work like *Kitāb Bātanjali* allowed for a freedom to select, evaluate, create, and translate within an Islamic frame what is manifestly a non-Islamic sphere of debate, where questions of self-justification and personal faith were simply irrelevant.

Thus, the possibility of such great freedom in the intellectual analysis of Hindu philosophy, and of such a degree of fascination for Hindu doctrines, may only have been possible because of al-Bīrunī's success in setting his chosen material within an Islamic interpretative and terminological framework. The clarity of the distinction he makes between an Islamic view (rather than an Islamization) of Hinduism and Islam itself may have actually engendered in him and his readers a deeper interest in and a more constructive engagement with Hindu philosophy and psychology. Furthermore, this engagement is a significant, perhaps even subversive contribution to the occasionally intense philosophical and psychological debates in the contemporary Arabic intellectual sphere. For example, in *Kitāb Bātanjali*, as cited in the *Hind*, liberation "is the return of the soul in a state of knowing to its nature" (§78.2). In the *Hind*, this concept is further sharpened:

> The soul's salvation, then, is through knowledge when it [the soul] understands things so as to define them

> comprehensively and specifically, without the need for deduction and without doubt, because when it categorizes existents by means of definitions, it perceives its own entity and [grasps] that it possesses the nobility of permanent existence, whereas matter possesses the ignominy of change and finitude in appearances.[28]

This concept is reminiscent of the Greek-Arabic terminology of contemporary philosophical debate where the soul reasons its own existence. This is clearly illustrated in the following citation from Ibn Sīnā's famous *Cure* (*Shifā'*): "We say, the soul reasons by taking into its own entity the appearance of intelligibles stripped of matter."[29]

Therefore, al-Bīrūnī's contribution to contemporary Muslim discussions on the nature of the soul in *Kitāb Bātanjali* should not be discounted on the grounds that he treats this subject within non-Islamic boundaries—on the contrary, his treatment does in fact occur within an Islamic context. It is precisely this novel use of Hindu psychology from an Islamic viewpoint, as a vehicle for philosophizing inside his cultural milieu, that is worth considering. It may be helpful to think not in terms of a process of "Islamization," but rather in terms of a terminological assimilation through the act of translating yogic terms from Sanskrit into Arabic, that enabled al-Bīrūnī to provide a culturally amenable philosophical and intellectual space for scientific investigation. This afforded him, his readers, and discussants the freedom to engage with and even assimilate certain foreign ideas while avoiding a conflict with their Islamic beliefs. Notwithstanding such an approach, the reading of Hindu psychology in *Kitāb Bātanjali* represents an accurate reflection of Patañjali's Yoga, even by modern scholarly standards.

Kitāb Bātanjali has as its main subject Patañjali's philosophy of the soul, which conveys a pragmatic and experiential approach to attaining salvation. This is accomplished by dealing with the whole individual as both spirit and matter, an approach whose practical degree of sophistication moves beyond the theoretical level of dualistic finality to the possibility of true liberation through unification. As such, the eight-limbed path of Yoga (*aṣṭāṅga yoga*) is expounded at length in Chapters Two and Three of *Kitāb Bātanjali*, addressing the physical, moral, psychological, and spiritual dimensions of the individual, using the terminology of contemporary Arabic philosophical debate.

Kitāb Bātanjali, then, is a reflection of the *Yoga Sutras*, in such a way that commentary—be it of al-Bīrūnī or of others—and text are woven into an integrated whole,[30] maintaining a close approximation of the general structure and progress of the Sanskrit *Sutras*. Al-Bīrūnī's reliance on the teaching of Patañjali over the teachings of others regarding the nature of the soul does more than signal his preference for one Hindu philosopher over another. It reflects a sensitive intellectual evaluation and Islamic synthesis by, for example, describing *īśvara* at the outset and throughout *Kitāb Bātanjali* in terms of the same attributes that Muslims use to describe God (§0.6, §12.2, §16.2). This synthesizing approach is initiated in *Kitāb Bātanjali* and concludes in the first ten chapters of the *Hind*.

By highlighting the theme of the soul–body relationship at the outset of *Kitāb Bātanjali* in practical, experiential, and personal terms, *Kitāb Bātanjali*, like the *Yoga Sutras* of Patañjali, translates the "universal," macrocosmic perspective into subjective, microcosmic terms. Yoga philosophy as described in *Kitāb Bātanjali* subtly addresses, and attempts to resolve, the tensions inherent in a dualistic perspective where *puruṣa* (soul) and *prakṛti* (matter) are separate and incapable of uniting. It develops an integration of being and positive (devotional) activity that as an embodied state reveals the essential difference between transmigration and reincarnation in existents.[31]

Conclusion

The intricacy of composition, translation, and allusion that permeates *Kitāb Bātanjali* creates a significant psychological and philosophical challenge for the reader. However, the lucidity and simplicity of the translation, despite the multiple layers in the Arabic of possible readings, influences, and reliance on unidentified sources, are an extraordinary tour de force given the Sanskrit text's level of sophistication. *Kitāb Bātanjali* is a testament to the remarkable intellectual abilities of its author and his thorough understanding of Hindu psychology and Yoga philosophy. As such, it marks an outstanding example of Hindu–Muslim intellectual encounters in the long and interwoven histories of these world religions.[32]

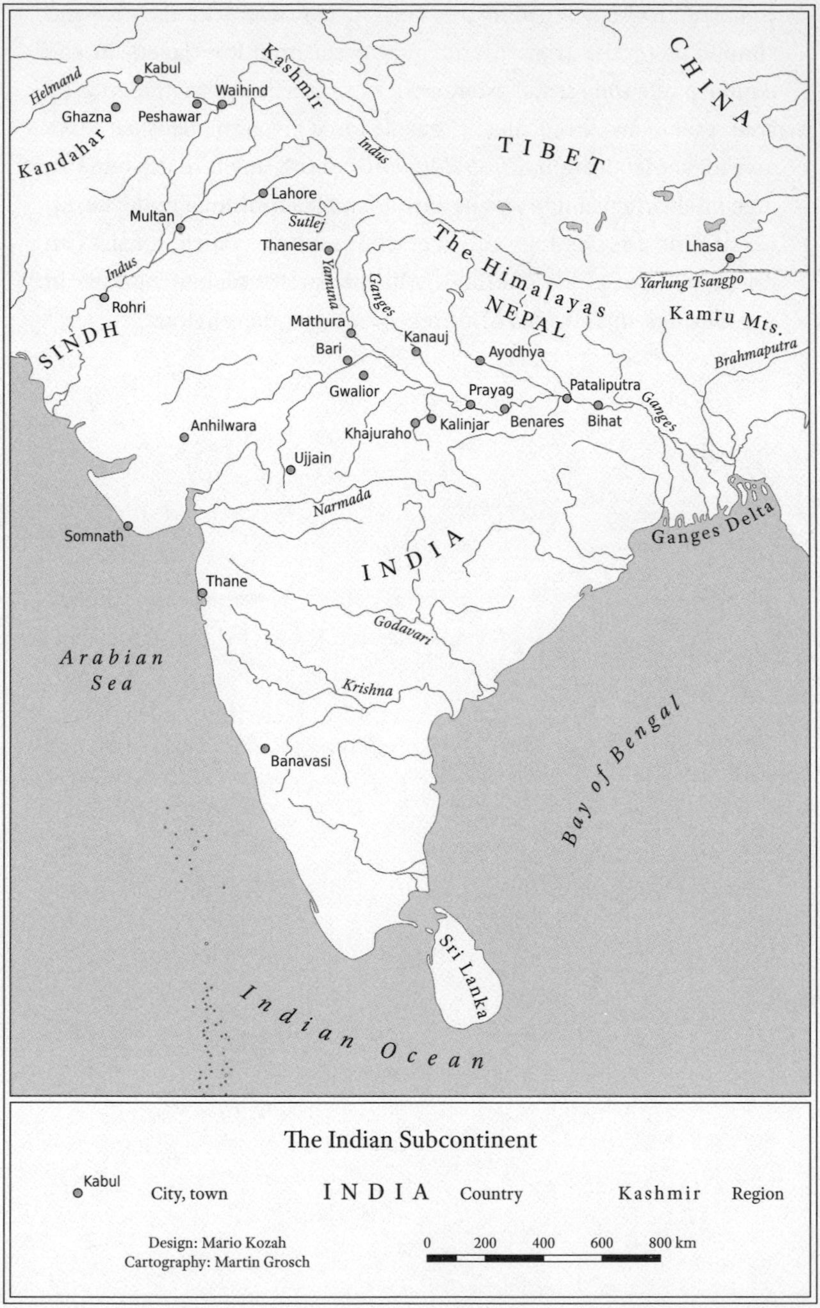

The Indian Subcontinent

Note on the Text

Previous Translations

There is only one previous translation of the *Kitāb Bātanjali*, which was published in four separate articles between 1966 and 1989 by Shlomo Pines and Tuvia Gelblum. It is entitled "Al-Bīrūnī's Arabic Version of Patañjali's 'Yogasūtra,'" and was published in the *Bulletin of the School of Oriental and African Studies*, University of London. The very scientific and literal translation is heavily annotated with fascinating and erudite points of discussion, sometimes running to several pages, while the translation itself is sometimes relegated to a mere three lines of a whole page. This makes it impracticable for the reader who wishes to appreciate the fullness and beauty of the text itself.

This Translation

The present translation has been established independently and only subsequently compared with earlier scholarly renditions. Careful attention has been paid to select the most appropriate terms for the Arabic philosophical and scientific terminology that al-Bīrūnī uses to reflect yogic concepts. This is because he rarely imports Sanskrit technical terms and concepts as loanwords but instead often employs Arabic philosophical terminology to express them. For example, wherever the term *karma* appears in the *Yoga Sutras*, it is consistently translated into Arabic as *iktisāb*, and rendered here as "acquiring *karma*," rather than just "acquisition."

Thus, this translation renders Yoga philosophy in terms resembling those through which Yoga philosophy is known in English already, rather than attempting to preserve the current conventions for English renderings of technical terms of Arabic science and philosophy. Given that al-Bīrūnī's Arabic text-commentary has its own inner dynamic, meaning, and independent logic, it is justifiable to translate some of the Arabic terminology used by taking into careful consideration the yogic technical implications of the term in an Arabic philosophical context. In this regard, the Glossary attempts to establish an approximate correspondence between the Arabic terms and meanings employed and the Sanskrit terms and meanings as they are rendered in the English translations of the *Yoga Sutras* available today, as well as in some of the major commentaries. This will help the reader trace the relationship between the Arabic and Sanskrit yogic terms. Al-Bīrūnī's consistency in the translation of these terms indicates an understanding of the subtle and interrelated nature of the terminology used in these *sutras*, and demonstrates that the Islamic and Arabic philosophical interpretative frame being applied is constantly and carefully maintained, both in the choice of specific terms used and in the contextual and psychological progression from *Kitāb Bātanjali* to the *Hind*.

Finally, a table of correspondences tracks the *sutras* in al-Bīrūnī's text to assist Indologists or students of Yoga who wish to compare the Arabic text with the Sanskrit original, or with the major commentaries available today.

Notes to the Introduction

1 For further biographical details see Bosworth, "Bīrūnī: Life," 274; Boilot, "Bīrūnī."

2 Al-Bīrūnī, *Kitāb Taḥqīq mā li-l-Hind*. Henceforth, the *Hind*.

3 Al-Bīrūnī, *al-Qānūn al-Masʿūdī*.

4 Al-Bīrūnī, *al-Āthār l-bāqiyah ʿan al-qurūn al-khāliyah*, 184.

5 Al-Bīrūnī and Ibn Sīnā, *al-As'ilah wa-l-Ajwibah*.

6 Kozah, *The Birth of Indology*, 11.

7 A Persian Muslim dynasty that ruled over Ṭabaristān and Jurjān from 319/931 to ca. 483/1090.

8 A powerful Persian Muslim dynasty of Turkic Mamluk origins that ruled large swathes of Khurasān, Afghanistan, and northwestern India from 366/977 to 582/1186.

9 "Al-Bīrūnī's Übersetzung des Yoga-Sūtra des Patañjali."

10 See Pines and Gelblum, "Al-Bīrūnī's Arabic Version of Patañjali's Yogasūtra."

11 Rosenthal, "On Some Epistemological and Methodological Presuppositions of al-Bīrūnī," 145.

12 Chapple, *Yoga and the Luminous*, 113.

13 Whicher, *Integrity*, 43.

14 Dasgupta, *Yoga Philosophy*, 39, 44.

15 *Hind*, 56, 65, 71, etc.

16 For possible influences, see Daiber, "Masā'il wa-Adjwiba" and Akasoy, "Philosophical Correspondence."

17 See the title to the work.

18 Flood, *An Introduction to Hinduism*, 126–27.

19 Kozah, *The Birth of Indology*, 107.

20 Whicher, *Integrity*, 348–49.

21 Kozah, *The Birth of Indology*, 116.

22 Kozah, *The Birth of Indology*, 120.

23 Kozah, *The Birth of Indology*, 125.

24 See Table of Correspondences in Appendix.

25 For a good English translation see Feuerstein, *The Yoga-Sūtra of Patañjali: A New Translation and Commentary*.

26 Hansbury, *John the Solitary on the Soul*.

27 Gallop, *Phaedo*.

28 *Hind*, 51.

29 Goichon, *Lexique*, 225.

30 *Kitāb Bātanjali*, §0.6: "Here begins the Book of Patañjali, with text and commentary interwoven."

31 For a full discussion of *Kitāb Bātanjali* see Kozah, *The Birth of Indology*.

32 For a full discussion of *Kitāb Bātanjali* see Kozah, *The Birth of Indology*.

The Yoga Sutras of Patañjali

Prologue[1]

The *Book of Patañjali the Indian* on liberation from afflictions, translated into Arabic by Abū Rayḥān Muḥammad ibn Aḥmad al-Bīrūnī. 0.1

People have different goals in life, and human society is ordered 0.2
by those differences. I am determined—totally dedicated, in fact—to educate others whenever I become satiated with learning, because I consider this to be the greatest happiness. Nobody who looks into the matter will blame me for the heavy work I continue to undertake as I translate from the Indian language for the benefit of friend and foe alike. Whoever disagrees with me will think me ignorant and regard the pleasure I derive as nothing but trouble. But every man has a specific interest and motivation. He will resist whatever his understanding cannot comprehend until he reaches a stage where he might be excused. Moral obligation applies only to what man has been given the means to perform.

I have translated books on arithmetic and astronomy from the 0.3
Indian language, and now I have gained access to works on philosophy held privately by their elite, and used by their renunciants to exert themselves on the path of devotion. When these books were read out to me word by word and I had understood their content, my conscience made me want to share it with other interested readers. For one of the ugliest crimes and worst sins is to withhold learning, because what is written in ink will always contain new information that, if known, will either draw some benefit or prevent some harm.

An Introduction about the Nature of the People and an Account of the Book

0.4 This is a people whose religious doctrines include basic propositions on transmigration and the sorrows of incarnation, as well as unification and generation not through the law of procreation. The result is that if you listen to their doctrines you sense a combination of beliefs found among the Ancient Greeks, Christian sects, and Sufi leaders. They all, without exception, maintain the belief that souls are bound in the world and tangled in its tethers, and that only those who reach the ultimate goal of liberation through strenuous effort are freed from these and achieve a permanent afterlife. Souls that do not reach this ultimate goal remain in the world and are reincarnated in entities, either good or evil, until they are refined and purified, bringing about liberation.

0.5 Their books are composed in meter, and these texts come with commentaries, making a complete translation in this format difficult. For the commentators focus a lot on grammar, etymology, and other areas that would only be useful for someone who knows their literary terminology well, not to mention the vernacular terms. This is the reason why I had to blend the text of my translation with the separate commentary, to set up the discourse as a dialogue consisting of questions and answers, and to remove topics related to grammar and language. I make this apology because of the discrepancy if one compares the size of the book in the two languages, and to keep anyone from thinking that this is the result of some deficiency in conveying the meaning. In fact, it is the outcome of a corrective revision. May God, by His grace, bestow felicitous success.

Here Begins the *Book of Patañjali*, with Text and Commentary Interwoven

0.6 I prostrate myself before the One who is above all else, and I give glory to the One who is the beginning and end of all things, who knows all beings. In turn, I magnify with humility of soul and purity of intention the angelic and spiritual beings that are below Him, seeking their support to accomplish the summary exposition I wish to make in the style of Hiraṇyagarbha.

In their writings, the ancients have extensively investigated what brings about the realization of the four objectives, which are: religion and mode of life, wealth and comfort, gratification and pleasure, liberation and permanence. In doing so, they barely left anything that could be discussed by those who came after them. What makes my exposition superior is that it clears up any ambiguity in their writing. It focuses on the means leading to the perfection of the soul through liberation from bondage, leading to the attainment of eternal bliss. I therefore state:

I hold that those objects that are not perceived should not be 0.7
characterized as imperceptible, except in certain cases, such as: those objects that are essentially small—for example, particles that cannot be sensed because of their minuteness; those that are far away because distance inhibits perception when its range is exceeded; what is blocked by a screen—for example, a wall preventing the perception of the object placed behind it, or bones that are sealed inside flesh and skin, or compositions of fluids within the body that cannot be perceived because of the barriers between us and them; their current absence, either because they existed before, such as bygone eras and extinct tribes, or because they will subsequently come to be, such as what is anticipated in the future; and deviation from methods of discovery that bring about full comprehension, as with the use of sound to determine the position of hidden objects in a cave. It is a well-known fact that complete certainty is only necessarily obtained by means of direct observation, and this is not possible with whatever is absent. The latter can only be evinced through attestations, and what is arrived at through evidence is not the same as knowledge acquired by direct observation. Similarly, logical demonstration dissipates uncertainty just as direct observation does. As long as misidentification impedes the soul, the soul remains in a state of confusion. It is unable to apply itself to

what effects liberation from this web and salvation from affliction and bondage, enjoying the status of immutability, in which birth and death do not occur.

0.8 In their books, the principal aim of theologians is to produce a discourse on which readers rely alone, or to guide them to a goal to which they find themselves drawn. These aims are specified by indications. Knowledge is divided into two parts: The superior part leads to liberation, because it is attainment of pure good, whereas the inferior part refers to those objectives that rank below this. For the benefit of the reader, I will strive to give my discussion of this obscure topic the certainty that comes with direct observation, as compared to the arguments set out by earlier authors.

Chapter One[2]

The renunciant, wanderer of the deserts and jungles, asked Patañjali: I have studied the books of the ancients and what they say about matters that lie beyond sense perception, and I found that they rely on weak and unreliable evidence. They do not use logical demonstration that is equivalent to direct observation, which brings with it cool certainty, opening the way toward the attainment of liberation from bondage. Could you therefore present me with logical demonstrations, along with evidence, of that goal to inform and aid me against uncertainty and doubt? 1.1

Patañjali: This is indeed possible, and I will elucidate the matter concisely using few terms that point to many meanings with the sound application of reason by analogy. Not everyone has a liking for or is able to engage with prolix expositions: They quickly lose interest in them, grow weary, and give up. Seeing that you have asked, now listen. What you are searching for is praxis: This has underlying causes, as well as results and consequences and an agent responsible for it. You need to have a proper understanding of each form of praxis, so you can examine critically the various teachings about it and to respond to related ideas. One part of praxis resembles action, while the other resembles the abandonment of action. When you understand this matter, you will discover the knowledge within it. It occurs when you withhold for yourself that which is dispersed from you toward external objects, so that it affects you alone. It also occurs when you prevent the soul's powers from attaching to 1.2

anything that is not you, and engage each of these powers in activity assigned to it from you. This action would then simultaneously encompass both knowledge and praxis.

2.1 QUESTION: What is the state of someone who has withdrawn his soul's powers into himself and restricted them from fluctuating outward?

2.2 ANSWER: He is not completely bound, having cut those illusory ties between himself and what is not himself, and ceased clinging to external objects. At the same time, he is not ready for liberation, since his soul is still with the body.

3.1 QUESTION: What state is he in if it is neither of the two you mentioned?

3.2 ANSWER: He would be as he truly is in essence.

4.1 QUESTION: This answer is not a satisfying explanation. Tell me whether he gains or loses anything accordingly, the way leather expands in the rain and contracts in the sun, which would mean that he is transitory and corruptible when exposed to successive states that change him; or whether he does not gain or lose anything, as with air, for example, which would mean he is inanimate and incapable of sensing things. Both views contradict the established definition of the soul as fundamentally animate, immortal, incorruptible, and permanent.

4.2 ANSWER: What I mean by my statement that he would be as he is, is that when these psychic senses and powers are withdrawn into him, they unite with him by attaching him to them and by his being a part of them. This individual perceived his surroundings through his senses and acquired knowledge of what is external to the soul through the powers that disperse from it. Consequently, he gains nothing when these senses and powers are withdrawn into him. He is now no different in this respect from how he was.

QUESTION: How many powers does the soul have that disperse from it? 5.1

ANSWER: There are five. The first is the power of apprehension, which occurs in three ways: either through the five senses; or by perceived inference from what is sensed, such as seeing smoke that indicates there is a fire hidden behind a wall; or by hearing information confirmed by general consensus, such as our knowing that the city of Kanauj is situated on the bank of the River Ganges. This is received knowledge that is equivalent to a person recognizing it visually. 5.2

The second is imagination, which is understanding something contrary to its true reality. One example is when the sun casts its rays on desert plains in a particular way and this is misconceived as water by a thirsty traveler. 5.3

The third is conjecture, which is not based on anything real. It reflects, instead, verbal formulations that are idiomatic and current. One example is when people say "the life of the spirit," which has no real meaning, but cannot be faulted given that it is in current usage. 5.4

The fourth is vision, which is when a person understands something that is virtual, and the entire state of that understanding has no actual reality. 5.5

The fifth is recollection, which is when the knower is able to recall a known object without being affected by forgetting. 5.6

QUESTION: How can the soul be restrained and its powers withdrawn from external objects? 6.1

ANSWER: This is achieved in two ways. The first is through praxis, which is practice. When a person engages with one of these powers within the soul itself, and exerts himself to curb its insubordination, allocating it a more befitting state and incessantly applying 6.2

himself to it for a long time, then, unless he repeatedly practices this, a degree of laxity may intervene, during which the soul may relapse into what is improper. However, through incessant application that eliminates with it agitation and multiplicity, that particular power will inevitably become firmly grounded in this practice and, consequent upon the cessation of habit, will cease its prior fanciful indulgences.

6.3 The second way is through dispassion, which is intellectual in nature. It is to contemplate undesirable outcomes with the mind's eye and consider the baseness of existents as decaying entities. Nothing, in fact, is worse than the transience and decay afflicting these existents. When a person comes to know the vile degradation of all objects, then this course will lead his mind to turn away from the ambitions of this world and the hereafter, freeing his mind to seek liberation from them, without being encumbered by inquiries and needs. These cause entanglement with what is in the world, further exacerbating bondage and inhibiting total commitment toward liberation. When his desire for all that is in the world disappears, he attains at this point a stage that transcends the three primary forces. No world, or even any existent, can exist without these forces since two of them constitute in their class both the generative and the destructive forces in nature. The third, intermediary, force draws on the other two, and as a result is capable of economy and control. He eventually transcends all three forces by retracting from them.

7.1 QUESTION: How many types of conception are there? One or more?

7.2 ANSWER: There are two types. The first is the conception of sensed material objects. The second is the conception of immaterial intelligibles.

8.1 QUESTION: Which one of them relates to self-deifying spiritual beings?

Answer: Since they do not belong to a compound class, they are bodiless. They therefore carry more of the second type in terms of value and worth than what is actually retained of it in people. 8.2

Question: How do angelic beings relate to these two types? 9.1

Answer: As with spiritual beings, they are restricted to the second type, free of the fear of being denied this state. All other spiritual beings, however, do not enter it with the same integrity and pureness due to the preoccupation with the consequences. 9.2

Question: Do angelic beings vary in superiority in this state or not? 10.1

Answer: They certainly vary in superiority, this being an inseparable attribute of all the spiritual and bodily classes. Consequently, the speed with which liberation is attained varies among them. The reason for this speed is undistracted engagement in action that leads to liberation. In contrast, its slow attainment is the result of half-hearted action. Therefore, they do indeed vary in superiority and differ in their stages. 10.2

Question: Is there a path to liberation other than the two paths of practice and dispassion? 11.1

Answer: Liberation may be attained by devotion, which is distributed in the body with understanding, certainty, and sincerity in the heart; with articulated exaltation, praise, and worship in the tongue; and with physical praxis in the limbs. All of this is directed exclusively toward God, in order to receive from Him the felicity of eternal bliss. 11.2

Question: Who is this object of devotion who grants felicity? 12.1

Answer: He is God, who through His primacy and unity has no need for action with its requital that takes the form of hoped- and 12.2

longed-for ease or feared and dreaded affliction. He is free from thoughts because He transcends hateful opposites and beloved likenesses. He knows through His essence eternally, for accidental knowledge occurs when something is not previously known, whereas He is not subject to nescience at any time or in any circumstance.

13.1 QUESTION: If someone who attains liberation is described as possessing these attributes, then how is he different from God, Exalted?

13.2 ANSWER: They are different because the one who attains liberation is and will be liberated in the future, but he was not so in the past, prior to attaining it. He is therefore like an imperfect warrior, given that he was unsuccessful during an elapsed period of time in the past, regardless of the state he has now attained. This is because his liberation is not pre-eternal, whereas God, Exalted, is possessed of these attributes in our three divisions of time: the past, present, and future. For in His essence He transcends time and the temporal from pre-eternity to future eternity.

14.1 QUESTION: Does He have attributes other than those you mentioned?

14.2 ANSWER: He is perfectly transcendent in scope, but not place, because He is beyond location. He is the pure and perfect good longed for by every existent, and He is flawless knowledge, uncontaminated by distraction and nescience.

15.1 QUESTION: Do you attribute speech to Him or not?

15.2 ANSWER: Given that He knows, He must undoubtedly also speak.

16.1 QUESTION: If He speaks on account of His knowledge, what difference is there between Him and the learned Kapila, and all other learned persons who have spoken on account of their knowledge?

Answer: Time is what makes them different. Those mentioned became knowledgeable and spoke after not having been knowledgeable in the past. They then conveyed their learning to others. Their speech and education are therefore in a specific time, whereas divine matters have no relation to time. Exalted God knows and speaks pre-eternally, and it is He who spoke in various ways to Brahma and other ancient sages. He delivered scripture to some, and opened a door for mediation with Him in others, and inspired a third group who acquired through thought what He had transmitted to them. 16.2

Question: Where did He acquire His knowledge? 17.1

Answer: His knowledge is eternally unchanged, and given that He was never nescient, His essence is knowing without having acquired any new knowledge. Accordingly, He says in the Veda that He revealed to Brahma: "Give praise and glory to the One who pronounced the Veda and existed before the Veda." 17.2

Question: How can one who is not apprehended by the senses be venerated? 18.1

Answer: Reciting His name substantiates His existence. For predicates are only given to actual things and names only to named objects. Although He is imperceptible to the senses and so they do not reach Him, the soul conceives of Him and thought comprehends His attributes. Through constant and rigorous engagement in this pure form of devotion, the effects of the aforementioned path of practice take place, barring those hindrances that prevent the soul from retracting into itself and restraining its faculties so as not to fluctuate outward and attach wrongfully. 18.2

Question: What are these hindrances that prevent the soul from turning in toward its essence? 19.1

19.2 ANSWER: The hindrances that prevent the soul from its true action, undistracted, are: blameworthy morals that come about by neglecting what is requisite; laziness in praxis; procrastination; doubt concerning what is right; inability due to nescience; and presuming that what is requisite is not so.

20.1 QUESTION: As a result of these hindrances, the soul acquires a deficiency. Are there other hindrances that are not blameworthy?

20.2 ANSWER: The soul is diverted by six types of concern: These include its anxiety, with fear-inducing thoughts that occur unintentionally; its fixation with a created being it expects to be incarnated into; its preoccupation with a frustrated desire and the depression that results; and its concern with changes in the body, its chariot, the symptoms of which forewarn it, or occur in it and through its actions.

21.1 QUESTION: What is the way to quash and to counteract these distractions?

21.2 ANSWER: By applying one's thought exclusively to God, Exalted, to the point of not being aware of or distracted by anything else.

22.1 QUESTION: What else must be intended alongside this prescribed type of thought?

22.2 ANSWER: He must want the well-being of all creatures, wishing for this without exception, and delighting when they attain it. He must show compassion to the wretched, the afflicted, and the distressed, and gladness for the works of the good and upright, and turn away from the actions of the evil and wicked. He must bring about a state of awareness in his soul, so that his breath would not dissipate in its two states of retention and expulsion.

QUESTION: What state is he in if he attains this stage before liberation? 23.1

ANSWER: His psychic power would have subdued his body, and, free of its corporeal hindrances, he would gain mastery over his soul. He can then choose to reduce and refine it to the size of a dust particle, or magnify it to become as expansive as air. He becomes like a crystal, in which surrounding objects can be seen as though contained in it, when in fact they are extraneous. Similarly, he will encompass his surroundings, so that when knowledge and what is known unite in him as the knower, then the intellect, intellector, and intellected all become identical for him. 23.2

Nevertheless, he advances through four stages of increasing sublimity and extremity. The first is the lowest, being the comprehension of the above three—the intellect, intellector, and intellected—as names, attributes, and undefinable particulars. When he surpasses this to arrive at definitions that transform the particulars of objects into universals, he attains the second stage. At this stage he continues to particularize in his understanding of objects. Then, when he ceases to particularize in his knowledge, apprehending objects as unified and time-oriented in their occurrence, he reaches the third stage. Here, when he experiences existence as differentiated from time and essence, he attains his knowledge of particulars and universals; then even what is as subtle as a dust particle cannot be hidden from him. He is superior to an informant who has missed a detail, making the latter's account unsatisfactory to the listener. Using names and attributes for designation becomes superfluous for him since these are the instruments of necessity and need. Accordingly, he reaches the utmost limit of the elevated fourth stage, and is worthy of being called "truth bearer."[3] 23.3

The first chapter of the *Book of Patañjali* is complete—
a book about concentrating the mind
on a single locus. 23.4

Chapter Two

Question: What is the path to that stage desired by someone slow who has not yet reached it? And how does one regain it after falling from it as a result of a lapse while there? 24.1

Answer: If the mind of the one who has lapsed had not been satiated, he would not have fallen from the joy he had attained. The way for a practitioner to reach this stage, or regain it in case of a lapse, is to continuously engage in devotional practices, and to gain reward and recompense by exerting his body through fasting, prayer, praise, recitations, and all other means that direct one toward the exalted Godhead, bringing one closer to Him. 24.2

Question: What does a person gain through exertion, dispassion, and asceticism? 25.1

Answer: The cultivation of the soul and the settling of the mind into quietude come about through the attenuation of his afflictions. 25.2

Question: What are these afflictions that encumber the mind? 26.1

Answer: They are nescience, conjecture, desire, antipathy, and ties. Of these, the most general is nescience, serving as their source and basis. The majority of them, if not all, bring about a man's ruin, and have long been the cause of people's errors, leading to their undoing. In a dispassionate renunciant, however, they only 26.2

exist potentially and do not actually manifest themselves. This is comparable to seeds stored in a granary, which do not germinate, even though they carry the capacity for germination, or a trampled frog that will not survive out of water, even though it is still alive. These afflictions are attenuated by dispassion and asceticism, which weaken and shrivel them to the verge of being reduced to nothing. However, for a novice who is not yet dispassionate they are still intense, powerful, and manifest. If he manages to control and attenuate one of these afflictions, another will powerfully replace it and grow even worse. As a result, the elimination of one will make no difference to him.

27.1 Question: How do you define these powers that afflict someone's mind and corrupt him?

27.2 Answer: Nescience is to conceive something to be contrary to its true reality. It is seeing the impure as pure, pleasure as good, misery as comfort, and the earthly, turbid body as eternal, wrongly equating it with the human being, when the latter is actually the soul.

27.3 Conjecture is the misidentification of things such that no differentiation between them is made and are all imagined to be the same, as a result of resemblance. For example, one may wrongly assume that the embodied intellector and subtle intellect[4] are, in terms of existence, one and the same thing; or wrongly assume, by not differentiating, that the light emanating from vision and that of the sun or a lamp are identical.

27.4 Desire is to crave worldly luxuries and to focus on pleasuring the senses with, for example, roses and Andhra sandalwood, and by chewing betel leaves after eating as a digestive and to stimulate the appetite.

27.5 Antipathy occurs as a result of affliction and pain in the body, or sorrow and worry in the soul. This leads to aversion and the manifestation of antipathy upon subduing them by cutting off their causes.

Ties are a consequence of the will, among other factors. They include consequents, similar to the use of accessories by someone lusting after women, which is the only way to successfully win their confidence. These include offering them gifts at an encounter, keeping prim and perfumed when in their company, flirting with them to encourage them to be more forthcoming, and other ways to flatter them and win their affection. Another example of an abhorrent consequent is a fixation with predicting one's own death and the possible forms it might take. 27.6

When all these afflictions are strong and prevalent, they inhibit the mind from striving in the proper manner and finding relief from affliction. If, however, they are weakened through dispassion, asceticism, and abstinence, as described above, they resemble fried seeds that will not germinate if sown in the ground, and roasted frogs that cannot be revived if plunged into a watering trough. Their corrupt and corrupting action is canceled, and they cease to materialize. They are then dissolved like the subtle forms of the body upon returning to their genera. 27.7

QUESTION: What is the reason behind implementing the attenuation, separation, and elimination described above in these five gross powers? 28.1

ANSWER: It is the quest for liberation. For the soul will continue to acquire demerit and merit so long as these forces encompass and overwhelm it . . . .[5] including recompense through compensation and requital. Although in the other world they are imagined, in this world they are both sensed and known. For example, when Nandikeśvara earned Paradise by making many offerings to Mahādeva, the supreme angelic being, he was transported there in his bodily form to become an angelic being. Another example is when Indra, head of the angelic beings, fornicated with the wife of the *brāhmaṇa* Nahuṣa, and was cursed and metamorphosed from an angelic being into a serpent. As long as the soul is subject to the 28.2

requital it acquires as *karma*, it will inevitably remain entangled, and will not find liberation from the web in which it is caught up.

29.1 QUESTION: Does entanglement have any other cause, and how is requital located in it?

29.2 ANSWER: Nescience is what truly hinders liberation, whereas everything else that follows comes from it, even if they are the cause of bondage. Nescience, then, is their source and origin, and the only cause of entanglement. The soul in relation to these powers is comparable to a grain of rice encased in its husk. The grain remains predisposed to sprouting and ripening as long as it is within the husk, locked in a cycle of generation and birth. But when the husk is winnowed from it, these episodes cease, and it becomes fully fit to remain in a single state. Requital, on the other hand, is found within different types of existents through the soul's reincarnation in them, depending on their lifespan, long or short, and whether their life experience is one of pleasure or suffering.

30.1 QUESTION: What is the soul's state when it subsists between merits and misdeeds, becoming trapped in the cage of rebirth for reward or punishment?

30.2 ANSWER: It is reincarnated according to the ease and distress it has previously committed and perpetrated, oscillating between pain and pleasure.

31.1 QUESTION: Are all entangled souls, then, equal to each other in this, or do they differ in their states?

31.2 ANSWER: The superior soul experiences only distress and pain, since ease in this world is no more than distress in the next. The truth of the matter is that ease can hardly be acquired without sinning in some way. Furthermore, a discerning individual grasps the fluidity of good and evil. As a result, the ease he obtains through requital is transformed into distress.

QUESTION: What must he do then? 32.1

ANSWER: He ought to avoid anything that produces entanglement and generates a particular station[6] for him. 32.2

QUESTION: What are these? 33.1

ANSWER: If the knower does not disentangle himself from known objects, he exists with them and is therefore unable to liberate himself due to this connection between him and them. The truth is that this connection exists only because of some particular nescience preventing him from disentangling himself from them. 33.2

QUESTION: How is this the case? 34.1

ANSWER: The knower aims to identify which of the five elements are found in every known object he sees—namely, earth, water, fire, wind, and sky. Another aim of his is identifying the known object's qualification: whether it belongs to the class of pure good, pure evil, or a combination of both. This understanding is attained through the senses. Sense perception, however, is subject to error and therefore not real. What is not real cannot be known for certain, and what lacks certainty is covered by nescience. 34.2

QUESTION: How is one able to discern the class of a known object? 35.1

ANSWER: If it is knowledge, it belongs to the class of pure good; if it is praxis, it belongs to the intermediate, mixed class; and if it is inertia,[7] it belongs to pure evil. 35.2

QUESTION: What is the cause that necessitates the connection between the knower and the known? 36.1

36.2 ANSWER: Void of the known, the knower knows potentially in his essence, and this state of knowing is only actualized through the known. Indeed, what is known is only so for the sake of the knower, and this is the reason why the connection between the two is necessary.

37.1 QUESTION: If the knower is a knower only through the known, how can he exist in the locus of liberation where the known is absent?

37.2 ANSWER: It is in the locus of entanglement, far from true discernment, that the knower is a knower only through the known. Knowledge in this state resembles an illusion acquired through artifice and diligence. For here the known is veiled and hidden, whereas in the locus of liberation the covers are removed, the veils lifted, and the hindrances severed, leaving the knower's essence in a state of pure knowing.

38.1 QUESTION: How can one achieve separation rather than this connection?

38.2 ANSWER: As long as a knowable object remains unknown, the desire to know it continues to grow, until it is finally known, at which point that desire abates. Objects that are known through the senses do not have the same fixedness as intelligibles. When this is fully ascertained without any shadow of a doubt, the connection in question is terminated, and the knower disunites himself from known objects, entering into a state of aloneness and disengagement. This is the meaning of liberation.

39.1 QUESTION: What occurs to the knower in this state of aloneness and disengagement?

39.2 ANSWER: Seven things occur to him. Three of them are in the soul: immunity from committing sins and the removal of the causes of suffering, leading to the third, which is the achievement of complete cessation of activity. Four are in the body: conceiving pleasure as pain, the substance of pleasure as nescience, the understanding of its negative causes as necessary to fully comprehend this, and the result, which is the actual elimination of these causes.

QUESTION: How are these seven things attained? 40.1

ANSWER: They are attained through limbs that make the knower pure and holy. 40.2

QUESTION: What are these limbs and how many are there? 41.1

ANSWER: They are eight in number. The foremost is, generally speaking, abstaining from evil. More specifically, it is not harming any living thing, and refraining from lying, stealing, and fornication, as well as avoiding any association with this world. All these must be relinquished unconditionally, without exceptions such as specifying a time and a place. It is not enough to avoid committing them; one must also not command others to do so or be pleased with their perpetrators. Although there are many types of evil depending on their scale, form, and the quality of their motives, they all arise from greed, anger, or nescience. What is more, their forms differ on a scale ranging from extreme excess to severe deficiency. When things become known via their opposites and contraries, along with the knowledge that he who kills has, through nescience, caused pain and distress to the victim, then the requital for such an action will clearly also include its constituents—namely, nescience and suffering. This being the case, he who does not kill is recompensed with the opposite of these two. Furthermore, nothing inimical will attempt to harm him. Why would anything attack him when he considers any two antagonists to be equal, holding the same view and attitude toward both. He would not, for example, judge in favor of the snake against the mongoose or vice versa. Lying, on the other hand, is essentially abhorrent, whereas he who favors truthfulness 41.2

is rewarded in heaven's highest ranks. He who guards his soul from the demon of robbery and the depravity of theft is given the ability to see treasures both above- and belowground. He who keeps it from the defilement of fornication develops the ability to accomplish any extraordinary feat he wishes, his soul encompassing times and places. He who avoids interaction with the world will secure knowledge of the condition and situation of his past state before acquiring his present form.

41.3 The second limb is inner and outer holiness. He who intends to clean and purify the body finds that its contamination increases, causing him to revile and hate it and turn to the love of what is pure, thus preferring the soul over the body. He who fasts from food will temper his body, purify its members, and sharpen its senses. He who finds contentment free of greed will be relieved from toil and released from slavery. He who frequently invokes the angelic and spiritual beings establishes contact with them in this way, as they become familiar to him in his mind. He who devotes himself to the glorification and remembrance of God will reject anything other than God in his mind, reverting to and concentrating uniquely upon Him.

41.4 The third limb is stillness. Anyone who covets something will chase after it, which involves movement, and such desire-driven movement will dispel any relaxation of tension. By drawing his mind's attention away from all individual and collective objects, he cultivates genuine stillness. He thereby gains immunity from the harms of heat or cold, from the suffering caused by hunger and thirst, and from feeling any needs—a state of restfulness results.

41.5 The fourth limb is cutting off the flow of breath through inhalation and exhalation, then suspending both movements, as a diver in watery depths dispenses with air. The turbidity in the mind of one who accomplishes this disappears, enabling it to do whatever he wants.

41.6 The fifth limb is sense withdrawal, which leaves him with only an inner consciousness and bereft of the knowledge that behind the sense organ is a separate object. This enables him to fully control and possess the sense organs.

The second chapter is complete, providing practical guidance concerning what had been presented in the first chapter. 41.7

Chapter Three

The sixth limb is calmness and serenity, to allow the mind to concentrate on a single object. 41.8

The seventh limb is maintaining thought upon the object that 41.9
the mind is concentrating on, in a state of absorbed unity, without exposure to multiplicity that would cause division and dispersal into various stages, or diversion to another object.

The eighth limb is total commitment to its maintenance until 41.10
thought becomes unified with its intended object.

When these eight limbs combine in him and his soul has been 41.11
disciplined by progressing through the stages[8] . . . . and reaching what is subtle and elevated. These last three limbs at the outset of the third chapter differ, in a sense, from the first five because they are closer to the intellect than to the senses. They verge on conceiving the known abstracted from matter, which is apprehended through sensory ties.

Question: Will a person reach the goal he is seeking through 42.1
these three limbs?

Answer: His transit in them resembles a person's transition 42.2
through the flow of years from infancy to old age. Knowledge of them is, in fact, single, because it disperses from the knower to the known objects; only then is it marked by multiplicity. When he establishes it, cutting it off from the dispersal through matter, it becomes single again and, through the third limb, total. Still, he has

not yet reached the stage of conceiving the known abstracted from matter. The mechanism for reaching this stage is practice, as stated earlier.

43.1 QUESTION: How is he recompensed for persevering in his adherence to practice?

43.2 ANSWER: He is recompensed with an understanding of the past, the present, and the future.

44.1 QUESTION: Is knowledge of them single or is it tripartite?

44.2 ANSWER: It is single, just as clay is dust before being kneaded, and afterward becomes a jar. There is a single substance of "clayness" in the three states despite the change in form; a clayness that is apparent in some of them and hidden in others. Similarly, the form of this single knowledge differs depending on the varying forms of time in its tripartite division.

45.1 QUESTION: Is he recompensed with anything else in this world?

45.2 ANSWER: Names do not change when they recur between speech and intellection. A jar remains a jar whether it is called so or conceived as such. He who knows objects by their names and conceives them based on their definitions, acquiring the habit of making this distinction and reducing it to its reality, knows the speech of birds. He who acquires the habit of establishing knowledge and gathering it understands his past state before bodily incarnation, and understands the love and enmity in the minds of others as a totality, but without an understanding of the particular object of that love or enmity.

46.1 QUESTION: How does he perform wonders through his actions?

46.2 ANSWER: Through thought and willpower, for he will find requital and reward in whatever he applies his thought to and fixes his willpower upon, despite the fact that any reward below liberation is neither perfect nor purely good.

Thus, he who wishes to become imperceptible maintains his thought on the body, and on the beauty and ugliness, the length and shortness, and the shape and appearance of its form. He strives steadily to divert other people's gazes and suspend their sense of sight, becoming invisible to them as a result. Similarly, if he maintains his thought on speech and its suspension, his voice would disappear and no longer be audible even if he were to shout. 46.3

He who wishes to acquire knowledge of the circumstances of his own death, maintains his thought on praxis. His soul will suddenly become equipped to understand the unknown. 46.4

He who wishes to conceive of Paradise and Hell, or the angelic beings and Hell's guardians, or his deceased ancestors, should maintain his thought on them while shutting out any sounds from resounding inside his ears, and blocking out the sight of any visible objects. 46.5

He who wishes to fortify his soul should always be mindful to delight in good and avoid evil, while showing compassion toward the evildoer. 46.6

He who wishes to fortify his body directs his thought in relation to it toward power and its centers. By maintaining this constraint, he acquires a power no less than that of an elephant. If he then directs his thought toward the light of the senses, after they have been subdued and restrained, he is recompensed with an understanding of the subtleties of present and hidden objects. 46.7

He who directs his thought toward the sun is recompensed with knowledge and vision of everything in the worlds. 46.8

The commentator at this point provides an explanation describing the world and its regions. It is worthwhile citing this fully, as it is one of the sciences in wide circulation among the renunciants. He begins by describing existents from the lowest region to the highest, setting darkness at the lowest point, measuring in *yojanas*—the 46.9

equivalent of 32,000 cubits in their system of measuring distances or eight miles in ours—one *koṭi* and eighty-five *lakṣas*. In our calculations this totals 18,500,000. For a *koṭi* in their numeric system is the name for ten million and a *lakṣa* for 100,000.

46.10 The commentator continues by stating that above the darkness is Naraka, or Hell. It measures thirteen *koṭis* and twelve *lakṣas*, which is 131,200,000 *yojanas*. Above Hell is further darkness, measuring one *lakṣa*. Above this darkness is a land called Vajra, or "thunderbolt," because of its hardness: It measures 34,000 *yojanas*. Above it is Garbha, or "the middle land," of 60,000 *yojanas*. Above it is Suvarṇa, or "the golden land," of 30,000 *yojanas*. Above that is Sapta Pātāla, or "the seven lands," each of which measures 10,000 *yojanas* . . . . The highest of them is the land of the *dvīpas*. The most central island is Jambu Dvīpa, which we inhabit. Then come Plakṣa Dvīpa, Śālmali Dvīpa, Kuśa Dvīpa, Krauñca Dvīpa, Śaka Dvīpa, and Puṣkara Dvīpa. Jambu Dvīpa measures one *lakṣa*, and those that surround it measure two then four *lakṣas*, continuing to double in this way until the farthest one is reached.

46.11 An ocean divides each pair of these islands—that is, lands. That which surrounds the one we inhabit is Kṣāra, or "the Salty"; then Ikṣu, or "Sugarcane Water"; Surā, or "Wine"; Sarpis, or "Clarified Butter"; Dadhi, or "Curds"; Kṣīra, or "Milk"; and Svādūdaka, or "Sweet Water." The first of these oceans is Kṣāra, measuring two *lakṣas*, with the rest doubling progressively as mentioned.

41.12 Beyond the "Sweet Water" ocean is Lokā Loka, or "the Uninhabited Land," measuring 10,000 *yojanas*. After it comes the Land of Gold, measuring ten *koṭis*. Above it is Pitṛ Loka, or the gathering place of the ancestors, measuring sixty-one *lakṣas* and 34,000 *yojanas*. Above it is one half of the Brahmāṇḍa egg—namely, that stationary half which contains the heavens. Above Brahmāṇḍa is a darkness called *tamas*, measuring one *koṭi* and eighty-five *lakṣas*.

46.13 In the middle of the island on which we find ourselves is Mount Meru, inhabited by angelic beings. One of the sides of its quadrangular shape measures five *koṭis*, and there are mountains, kingdoms, rivers, and seas on its four sides. It would not be worthwhile enumerating or naming them all, given that they are unknown and in Sanskrit.

The commentator then enumerates the *lokas*, regions, stating that the Bhūr Loka is inhabited by humans, beasts, and birds, with mountains, rivers, and trees. It reaches up to the sun in its extent. He then lists Bhuvar Loka, in which the sun Vishvadhara is to be found, extending up to the polestar. Then Mahar Loka, which is the abode of the world's guardians, such as Indra and others like him. Then Jana Loka, which includes masters from among the various types of angelic beings. Then Tapo Loka, in which the *bharata-kumara* are found. Then Satya Loka, which is the location of the recompensed *brāhmaṇas*, called Brahma Deśa for this reason, just as the location of the recompensed Kshatriyas is called Rāja Deśa. Then Brahma Loka, where Brahma is found. These seven *lokas* measure fifteen *koṭis* in total. All together they are called Brahmāṇḍa, just as we call the entirety of the celestial spheres ether. 46.14

The commentator's explanation ends here. Let us now return to the text. 46.15

Patañjali: Whoever directs his thought toward the moon attains knowledge of the arrangement of the stars, their positions and functions. 46.16

He who directs them toward the polestar, which is a constellation of fourteen stars in the shape of a *śakvara*, great lizard, or a *safan*, a reptile whose rough skin is used to produce sword hilts, acquires knowledge of the stars' movements. Thus, whoever wants one of those things we have mentioned will acquire it if they have applied their thought to it. 46.17

He who wishes to understand his own body should continuously direct his thought to the navel. 46.18

This is also from the commentator's explanation: When food is processed in the belly, a substance is produced from it consisting of 46.19

loose sediment and three residues, which remain in the body. These are wind, bile, and phlegm, which in turn harm seven things: chyle, blood, flesh, fat, bones, marrow, and semen.

46.20 The substance mentioned above is transformed into blood, generating flesh from its fine matter, while producing from its gross matter everything that emerges from the body, such as sweat, hair, nails, and so on. Then fleshy fat is generated from the flesh, bones from the fat, marrow from the bones, and from the marrow semen, which is the finest of these. The further from this substance, the more excellent the product is. Understanding how these things transform, how they are generated and decompose, how they are useful or harmful, and knowing the times and periods in which they occur, has the single benefit of confirming that none of it is good; on the contrary, it is all evil. This in itself is a cause drawing one to what is good. We now return to the text.

46.21 He who wants to remove the harm that occurs to him from hunger and thirst should direct his thought toward the hollow part of the chest and the throat, which is the course of wind in respiration.

46.22 He who wants to achieve motionlessness should contemplate the "tortoise," which are those twisted veins above the navel similar to it.

46.23 He who wants a vision of the siddhas—renunciants able to attain the goals desired, becoming invisible through knowledge and virtue, and inhabiting Bhuvar Loka—should direct his thought toward the light in the hole of the vertex bone. By doing so, he will actually see them with his eyes.

46.24 He who wants to acquire knowledge should direct his thought toward the mind, its source and place, conceiving it as indistinguishably united with the soul, given that the soul knows and the mind lives. He would not encounter any difficulty in doing so after having completely disengaged his thought from this world, thereby obtaining understanding of his essence in its true reality, without any sensed objects being undisclosed to him, even if they are absent and remote.

QUESTION: Is there anything superior to this requital that comes through knowledge? 47.1

ANSWER: Why would there not be, given that this knowledge is unreal, and a hindrance from true knowledge? We have already presented the results of theoretical knowledge as one part. Let us now discuss the results of the other part, which is practical knowledge. For the renunciant described, one who has attained the distinction of praxis combined with knowledge is on the verge of obtaining what is desired. Should he wish to transport himself from his own body to another—without his spirit and while still in this state of entanglement, but not in the way this occurs after death; rather, by his own free will, decision, and choice—then he is able to do it. The reason is that bodies are the nets of spirits, recompensing them for earlier acts of good and evil with corresponding ease or distress. Procuring the former and dispelling the latter will inevitably involve some mistreatment and aggravation toward one's own species or the other species, necessitating future recompense. However, the renunciant in question has fulfilled his dues for past actions in his present form and withdrawn from acquiring any more *karma* for the future. In this case, there is no necessitating factor, and he knows where his soul has come from and where it is going. He is therefore able to move and maneuver it unconstrained by the body in which it moves freely. This is also the reason he can die of his own volition whenever he wishes. 47.2

QUESTION: Is he able to move this bodily garment with him through praxis of which others are incapable? 48.1

ANSWER: Were his bodily state similar to that of ordinary people with respect to its density and sediments, he would have been incapable of having it accompany him. In actual fact, its state is devoid of any sediments and residue. 48.2

Five types of wind are found in the body. Two of these are within 48.3
the respiratory tract, of which one enters through inhalation, while

the other exits through exhalation. The third wind is located in all parts of the body, being one of its four elements. Movement such as leaping and motion occurs through the fourth wind, while the fifth is circulatory, carrying nutrients and various mixtures from one part of the body to another. As a result, no single part remains in a permanent state.

48.4 If this renunciant masters the leaping wind, maintains his thought upon it, and fortifies it through enhancement, then his supported weight is reduced. He would then be able to walk on flowing water and shifting mud as someone else might on solid ground, without drowning or sinking. He would also be able to step on sharp thorns with his bare feet without them being pierced, the result of the absence of supported weight that would have exposed him to their harmful effects. This wind is found in various measures among walking and flying animals such as the antelope and the tortoise, or the chicken and the pigeon. The difference in measure within each pair of the same species from one of these two categories can reach opposite extremes.

48.5 So too, if he fortifies the wind that carries mixtures, his body would appear to others aflame like a blazing fire. Furthermore, hearing occurs through the air because it is a part of it. When the renunciant attains a true understanding of the two by focusing his thought on both, he hears sounds that occur in the air even if they are spatially far from him.

48.6 Moreover, since the body is heavy and air is light, when his thought combines the two, this renunciant's body becomes as light as plant particles that float around in the air's currents; his weight is not penetrated by the air, allowing him to fly to whichever ends of the Earth he wishes, lighter than the flight of birds.

49.1 Question: Do all these abilities combine in a single individual or does each renunciant have one particular accomplishment?

ANSWER: All these abilities combine in a single renunciant because thought is one; and this combiner is called mahāvideha. If he contemplates his own body, uniting with the air, he is able to fly because of its lightness. If union takes place with fire, he becomes effulgent from its light. He obtains what he intends and desires from whichever natural bodies he contemplates, because each of these bodies consists of three states. The first of them is identity; for example, the Earth consists of "earth." The second state consists of those entities created out of "earth," but that differ from it in form; for example, minerals and plants. The third state is its essence; for example, the characteristic of earthiness commonly found in it and in its derivative objects. 49.2

If he investigates the universals as well as the particulars within elements, the renunciant becomes capable of canceling their harmful effects on his body, such as not being burnt by fire, or penetrated by air, or drowned by water, or hindered by earth, and other similar examples. He has the power to refine his body, making it visible or invisible whenever he wants. He can also make it beautiful or ugly, or fortify, soften, coarsen, or harden it, allowing him to appear in any form he wishes. He can make it light enough to fly, dive, skim along the ground, and soar. He can make it gigantic, terrifying anyone who sees him. He has the power to perceive an object using his senses, even if it is distant from him. Nothing can hinder his passage, or move him when he is motionless. How can things affect him when he has the power to destroy and create them; when in fact they are under his command? 49.3

QUESTION: This is what manifests in him in terms of the five elements of earth, water, fire, wind, and sky. But what of the incorporeal that manifests in him? 50.1

ANSWER: We have already stated that the renunciant's senses become purified by overcoming hindrances, which cannot then forcefully disable the senses' process of perception. He is, in fact, 50.2

able to see without using his eyes and hear without using his ears. He transcends the three primary forces, which are pure good, pure evil, and their intermediary, with all three then falling under his will, for none of them occurs in another, apart from his efforts. The basis for this condition is the discernment of the true reality of the body, the mind, and the soul. When this occurs, everything falls under the renunciant's supremacy, to the point that he understands them by their definitions and is omniscient regarding them,[9] and comprehends them as universals.

51.1 QUESTION: Can the renunciant attain the same highest stage through this knowledge as he can through actions?

51.2 ANSWER: No, because the one who has this knowledge, even if it is termed such, falls short of liberation were he to consider it a type of knowledge, for it is acquired through the senses. In fact, knowledge is an understanding of the obliteration and dwindling of known objects, followed by its rejection. Just as what is assumed to be knowledge actually prevents liberation, so too boasting and showing off about it, which is a sort of pretentious superiority, will prevent its attainment. Angelic beings who reveal themselves to the renunciant will offer him their state and status, and invite him to Paradise. They will describe it to him as the source and storehouse of everything that is good, including all the trees and fruits that might possibly come to mind, as well as women, the very sight of whom affords every joy and ease. It is free from any harmful heat or cold, and the one who lives there is immune from infirmity, diseases, and all other physical ailments and base needs. Such an invitation may result in this renunciant's soul becoming bloated with the signs of its own pride. He will, as a consequence, revert to a lower stage of existence, and his commitment will be deflected.

52.1 QUESTION: How should he respond to the angelic beings so as to be saved from this outcome?

ANSWER: He should respond by saying that the man of this world is like a worm in a great jar filled with blazing coals. The coals represent this world, in which suffering results from the distress and turmoil that occur here, without any hope of release and deliverance from it. This was the state I was in as I clung to the world, but when I withdrew from it, I abided in the shadow of death, obtaining a small measure of relief from toil and fatigue. At what point, then, would my mind incline toward Paradise, and why would I wish to be preoccupied with its delights? For the outcome would be reverting back to bondage, and I would thereby have squandered all the effort I had put toward reaching liberation. 52.2

QUESTION: What is true knowledge, if what has been presented above is not? 53.1

ANSWER: It is found within the quantum of time present, by which I mean its current moment. 53.2

QUESTION: What is attained by it? 54.1

ANSWER: An understanding of the essence and class of a thing is attained, followed by its quality—or what distinguishes it from other objects—followed by its spatial location, state, and direction. 54.2

QUESTION: What is this knowledge, its object, and its qualification called? 55.1

ANSWER: This knowledge is called the "traverser" and "crossing." Its object is everything that is either completely refined or dense, and its qualification is the universal mixtures, as in a unified whole through a single species. Furthermore, it is only beneficial when applied, by encompassing the sensed and known objects, and differentiating itself from them at the foundation. 55.2

56.1 QUESTION: When does liberation occur?

56.2 ANSWER: A person's soul is a pure and unblemished divine substance, and the reason the mind is defiled is because it fluctuates between the three aforementioned primary forces. As long as the mind has not yet attained the same state of purification as the soul, allowing them to unite through this shared attribute, then their mixing together is of no benefit and liberation does not occur.

56.3 The third chapter on the specific topic of recompense and how to obtain requital is complete.

Chapter Four

Question: You said earlier that the state of renunciation is only attained by the renunciant either through devotion carried out with a pure and immaculate mind, with sincere intention, and holiness in one's praxis, or through withdrawal from the objects of sense perception and the control of the senses. Can this condition be attained in any other way? 57.1

Answer: It may be attained in one of five ways: The first is for the individual to perform many good deeds in this world and to worship God for a long period. However, he will not attain this state of renunciation in the form he is currently in but only when he is transported through death and prepared for a form in which he can enjoy that state. The second is for him to perform many good deeds and augment his devotional practices, as a result of which God will grant him the grace of wisdom while he remains in his current form, as well as the splendor of this state of renunciation. The third is for him to attain it by ingesting *rasāyana*, which are drugs and medical treatments prescribed for this purpose. The fourth and fifth ways are those stated at the outset. 57.2

Question: Is it possible for the renunciant you have described to become a spiritual being? 58.1

Answer: When he is in his bodily form he cannot transport himself to that level. But when he separates from his form, and if this state of separation persists and he opts to intensify one of the three 58.2

primary forces, then he will be delivered to the class whose force he had intensified, becoming either an angelic being or a devil or a jinni.

59.1 QUESTION: By intensifying one of these three forces, does he acquire a reward or commit a sin, warranting a bodily incarnation of the class he desires?

59.2 ANSWER: This intensification is not to acquire anything but simply a love of change, so that if he intensifies the good force, he will remove evil from his soul and become an angelic being, and if he intensifies the evil force, he will remove good from his soul and become a devil. This is comparable to someone who irrigates his crop, leading to excess water gathering unintentionally in one part of it. He then proceeds to dig a channel to siphon it off, not in order to irrigate, but simply to remove this excess water from his crop.

60.1 QUESTION: If this renunciant is able to magnify what is small, increase what is scant, and transform his body into many bodies, assisting each other in the pursuit of one aim, would these exist with many minds or with one or with none? The latter option would necessarily make them lifeless corpses; the middle option would necessitate action in only one of them, since the mind reflects at first, and then the body acts accordingly; and if they exist with many minds then disparate thoughts would arise, leading to divergent actions.

60.2 ANSWER: Each of them has its own mind but none possesses anything that the other does not, making them different from one another; rather, they are bodies and minds that issue from him. The source, then, is the first body and the rest are dependent on it.

61.1 QUESTION: Which of the above five ways to attain the state of renunciation is the most preferable?

Answer: The final, fifth one, which is the possession and restraint of the senses. 61.2

Question: If this state of renunciation is common to those who employ any of the five ways then what is the purpose of singling out the last of them as excellent? 62.1

Answer: Because those who employ the first four ways are either gaining reward or committing sin or something in between such that their minds are distracted by recompense and requital for acquiring *karma*, whereas the renunciant who employs the fifth way truly has a clear mind. What a difference there is between one who is free of something and one who is preoccupied by it! 62.2

Question: If a person has acquired *karma*, necessitating requital, while in a form that is not the one in which the acquiring of *karma* had taken place, does the long period of time between the two conditions result in the matter being forgotten? 63.1

Answer: Praxis accompanies the soul because it is the soul's action and the body is its instrument. There is no forgetfulness with matters relating to the soul because it lies outside time and it is time that determines what is recent and distant in terms of duration. By accompanying the soul, this praxis transforms its nature and innate disposition so as to resemble that state to which it transitions. For the soul in its purity knows this, remembers it, and does not forget it. What veils the soul's light is the body's turbidity when it combines with it. 63.2

Question: If the evildoer transmigrates to another evil state, he will acquire through the move a doubling of the evil act. Does this process have a definite limit requiring it to stop or not? 64.1

Answer: The limit is unknown to us even if it exists. However, we do see that juveniles and children are happy when long life is 64.2

invoked for them and are saddened when a hasty end is invoked. What meaning would these two invocations have for them had they not savored the sweetness of life and experienced the bitterness of death in previous cycles in which they had transmigrated for reasons related to requital?

65.1 QUESTION: If a beginning for this process is not known, and the individual is locked in a cycle of acquiring *karma* and recompense, then that action within the body becomes natural for him so that an end to it is also not known. This leads to his being cut off at the root from attaining liberation.

65.2 ANSWER: Were it not that this action has a cause that produces and drives it, then the point would have been as you conceived it. However, you know that action has conditions that drive it, so that when these are removed, the action will also cease and reach its end and culmination, facilitating the path in the quest for liberation. Because the mind is inconstant in its remembrance of the end and is preoccupied with the recompense prepared for it, sometimes desiring its ease and sometimes dreading its affliction, since recompense is canceled by removing what necessitates reward or sin, then what, I wonder, is the mind attaching itself to at that time if not to desire or dread, since it is only an absence of preoccupation that enables it to seek liberation. As long as they are both present and unremoved then the issue will center on acquiring *karma* within bodies in an uninterrupted manner even if the individual does not remain in a single state or similar ones; rather, both types—good and evil—are transformed, the one into the other, through exchange or mixture. Thus, sometimes a person is rewarded with a benefit but then commits an offense as a result of moving from body to body; and harming others is necessarily a sin. Similarly, when a person is being punished for wickedness and certain sentiments of mercy or benevolence arise in him while in that body, then this necessitates reward. If good and evil are not both annulled simultaneously, then a cessation of activity will not occur, nor will the cycle be broken. However, this particular renunciant has annulled both in the future and they in themselves have regressed to the past, becoming annihilated, or almost so, and for this reason he has secured the goal of liberation.

QUESTION: If good and evil are both annihilated in his past and in his future but liberation leaves an effect, then how can an effect be produced from two nils? 66.1

ANSWER: They are not totally annihilated; rather, there is a transition into potentiality or a potential existence in two specific periods of time so that they have no real effect on actual existence in the present. This is similar to when what is white becomes yellow, and yellow then becomes black: While in the state of yellowness, the white and the black are not totally annihilated, for otherwise their existence would have changed. However, what then comes is in a state of potentiality relative to them both, so that even if their existence is too subtle to be felt by the senses, it is not too subtle to be perceived by the intellect. Furthermore, both are formed by the three primary forces. Proof of this is that when the past was present it was not devoid of requital—the cause of which was those forces—just as the future, when it becomes present, will not be free of them either. Both present and past, therefore, have an effect, for otherwise they would not impact existence. 66.2

QUESTION: If the three primary forces mutate and become different, is it then possible for them to come together in a state of unification? 67.1

ANSWER: Why should this not be the case, given that the oil, the wick, and the fire of a lamp function differently, but when their effects are combined and their actions united the lamp burns with a single light? For the same reason, when the mind is purified and the soul disciplined so that they exist together, then the intelligible, 67.2

the intellect, and the intellector are united, and they all become an intellector.

68.1 QUESTION: What is the meaning of "the intelligible" when the intellect intellects and what it has intellected unites with it, for this can only lead to the conclusion that nothing other than the intellect exists?

68.2 ANSWER: Just as you only recognize the Truth, so we only recognize the intellector. Ultimately, there is no difference in meaning between us; rather, the difference lies in the expression. The meaning of "unification," as it stands, transpires within a single given, just as a wife's parturition is called "the camel's milking time" by her husband when he conceives of her in labor, whereas he conceives of her after a beating as inimical, due to his excessive jealousy, and then calls her "loathsome," while some wives are given a form of equality in marriage where the husband calls her "partner," and similar examples in which the meaning is the same but the name differs. For when intellect exists on its own, the necessary consequence is that only knowledge and understanding are perpetual. We do observe, however, that known objects may often become unknown, from which we can deduce that the difference between these two states is brought about by an intellector who intellects by means of an instrument he has—namely, the intellect. The intellect knows a thing when it is present, and that thing is concealed from the intellect when it is absent. The intellect knows a thing, then another thing presents itself, which becomes known, and the understanding of the two corruptible things is itself subject to corruption, for there is a difference between them. If there was nothing other than the intellect then there would be a single perpetual understanding of all things. However, the intellect in relation to the intellector is like a gem positioned between one's eyes and an object of sight; when it shines, it sends the colors and forms of what is seen to the seer.

QUESTION: So, is the intellect like a lamp in the way it reveals itself, needing nothing besides itself? 69.1

ANSWER: As the lamp is for someone seeking light, so is the intellect for an intellector. 69.2

QUESTION: Given that the intellect perceives itself and by itself, does it, as a result, need anything other than itself? 70.1

ANSWER: Its perception is not of itself, since that which is collected does not collect itself but something else does so. The intellect only perceives after a stimulus to perception, and it only perceives an intelligible. Therefore, the imprint of something other than itself and some form of collection take place within it. The intellector is different, for it is unification rather than collection that takes place within him. Thus, your view is invalidated and what we have said is correct. 70.2

QUESTION: What is the fruit of secret knowledge? 71.1

ANSWER: Its fruit is the removal of desire and the desired. 71.2

QUESTION: What benefit is there from the removal of this desire? 72.1

ANSWER: The attainment of the middle path toward knowledge such that it eradicates desire and makes real unicity for the One, the Truth. 72.2

QUESTION: Does there remain in the one who attains this exalted desire any residue of worldly filth or is he purified from the stain of nescience? 73.1

ANSWER: For a person in this world, nescience is as it were the natural state, while knowledge is accidental and foreign to him. Thus, a residue of what is innate and customary is inevitable upon the onset of what is extraordinary. 73.2

74.1 QUESTION: How can he be smelted so as to be completely purified of nescience?

74.2 ANSWER: Through practice, meditational praxis, and physical exercise, the method of which was described earlier. When he gradually becomes habituated to what is required, the habit will become like nature, at which point its action will overcome nature and the practitioner will be purified of that residue. On reaching this stage, he removes himself from the motives of both reward and sin, becoming cleansed of impurities. Knowledge then establishes itself in a measure that does not increase through an influx of known objects that can no longer be either remote or accessible, for these are now annihilated through the unification of the three forces.

75.1 QUESTION: What would be the state of the three primary forces at that time?

75.2 ANSWER: The action of these forces is connected with time and duration, which are replaced by the joy that arises in someone who is truly happy. He thus transcends the three forces and no longer needs them.

76.1 QUESTION: What is the action's duration?

76.2 ANSWER: It is *kshana,* which is one-fourth of the blink of an eye.

77.1 QUESTION: How is the action's need for a specific duration known?

77.2 ANSWER: When what is colored white starts to go yellow, for the transition between these two colors cannot do without this duration.

78.1 QUESTION: How is liberation brought about?

78.2 ANSWER: It is possible to say that liberation is the suspension of the three primary forces from their action, returning to the source from which they came. You might also say that it is the return of the soul to its nature.

This concludes the fourth chapter on the subject of liberation and unification, and marks the end of the book consisting in its entirety of 1,100 inquiries[10] in verse. 78.3

Epilogue[11]

This was the *Book of Patañjali*. The present translation was required by the following consideration: The authors of books about the beliefs of the Indians neglected the subject of their religious paths. The result was that if the content of these books was used for debating with opponents, the discussants would have no point of reference, since the starting point of their debate would be disapproval and repudiation. He who does not recognize evil cannot avoid it, just as he who does not recognize good is unable to acquire it. This is the reason behind the saying "Learn magic but do not use it." 79.1

There are two reasons for the absurd propositions contained in the book. The first is that most communities that adhere to the basic tenets we have mentioned, concerning incarnation or unification—while being excessively vague in discussing details—state something the existence of which is rationally impossible. I will pass over those who regard as miracles worked by saints things similar to the preceding descriptions, and another group that, contrary to the first group, endorses these absurdities, conceiving of them as attacks on the miracles worked by the prophets, may God's prayers be upon them. Consider the Christians who are characterized the way we have described it: their excess in ascetic practices and withdrawal from the world, as witnessed by the prohibition against molesting those of them preoccupied in their cells with the suffering of their souls to such an extent that moisture evaporates from their bodies and no flesh remains between their skin and bones. One of them might even die while in a state of devotion, in an upright position 79.2

propped up on a staff against the wall for many centuries and eras as a result of the loss of dense matter and absence of rot and its causes inside his body. The dust preserves him and he achieves renown through commemoration and pilgrimage from all regions until desiccation achieves what moisture was unable to accomplish by dislocating his limbs and crumbling his bones, at which point he is gone.

79.3 As for their absurd tales, they will recount miracles to you when they mention the early fathers, the later bishops and patriarchs, and those martyred for the faith, and they will talk about the growth of their hair and nails after death, which would need cutting and clipping, invalidating astonishing tales told by others.

79.4 The second reason is that the Indians hold the greatest share of what is rationally impossible and tend the least toward critical examination and scientific study, to such an extent that I can only compare the concepts and the logical arrangement and organization of their books of mathematical astronomy to pearls mixed with dung, or to gems mixed with potsherds. They are not motivated to distinguish good astronomical ideas from bad ones and do not engage in refining and improving them. This is exacerbated by their practice of setting themselves apart from others and prohibiting association with them. Otherwise they would have certainly improved as a result of the objections of opponents and the refutation of their ideas. The only debates they hold are with the Buddhists who live among them and resemble them, but who are actually no better.

79.5 God willing, I will compose a book giving an account of their religious laws, explaining their beliefs, and identifying their terminology and narratives as well as certain features of their territory and realms. It will be a manual for those who wish to consort and converse with them, should God prolong my life and dispel the handicaps of illness and ailment.

79.6 This is the conclusion of the *Book of Patañjali*. Loftiest is God and more sublime with His eternal grace and favor. Have mercy, Lord, for You are indeed Merciful and Compassionate.

Appendix of Parallel Citations in the *Taḥqīq mā li-l-Hind*[12]

In the *Book of Patañjali* the path of liberation is divided into three. The first is functional through practice by gently drawing the outflowing senses back in so that their activity is entirely self-focused. §1

Furthermore, there is supporting evidence in the *Book of Patañjali* similar to what has been cited above[11] with reference to someone who has withdrawn his senses and feelings as a tortoise might retract its limbs when it is afraid. Such a person is not bound, having loosened his bonds, but at the same time is not liberated because he is still with his body. §2

The renunciant in the *Book of Patañjali* asked: Who is this object of devotion, through devotion to whom felicity is obtained? §12

Answer: He is the One, who through His primacy and unity has no need for action with its requital that takes the form of hoped- and longed-for ease or feared and dreaded affliction. He is free from thoughts because He transcends hateful opposites and beloved likenesses. He knows through His essence eternally.

They believe that liberation is achieved through unification because for God hope of requital or fear of strife is redundant. He is free from thoughts because He transcends hateful opposites and beloved likenesses. He knows through His essence, not through accidental knowledge of what He did not know in a particular circumstance.

§14 AFTER THIS, HE ASKED: Does He have attributes other than the ones you mentioned?

ANSWER: He is perfectly transcendent in scope, not place, because He is beyond location. He is the pure and perfect good longed for by every existent, and He is flawless knowledge uncontaminated by distraction and nescience.

§15 QUESTION: Do you attribute speech to Him or not?

ANSWER: Given that He knows, He must undoubtedly also speak.

§16 QUESTION: If He speaks on account of His knowledge, what difference is there between Him and the learned sages who have spoken on account of their knowledge?

ANSWER: Time is what makes them different. For they became knowledgeable and spoke in time after not having been knowledgeable in the past. They then conveyed their learning to others. Their speech and education are therefore in a specific time, whereas divine matters have no relation to time. Exalted God knows and speaks pre-eternally.

§17 QUESTION: Where did He acquire His knowledge?

ANSWER: His knowledge is eternally unchanged, and given that He was never nescient, His essence is knowing without having acquired any new knowledge. Accordingly, He says in the Veda that He revealed to Brahma: "Give praise and glory to the One who pronounced the Veda and existed before the Veda."

§18 QUESTION: How can you venerate Him who is not apprehended by the senses?

Answer: Reciting His name substantiates His existence. For predicates are only given to actual things and names only to named objects. Although He is imperceptible to the senses and so they do not reach Him, the soul does conceive of Him and thought does comprehend His attributes. Through rigorous engagement in this pure form of devotion felicity is attained.

The author of the *Book of Patañjali* stated: Applying one's thought exclusively to the unity of God engages one's awareness of something other than what one had previously been preoccupied by. §21

He who seeks God must also want the well-being of all creatures, without making a single exception for any reason. He who applies himself exclusively to his soul would not inhale or exhale for it. §22

At this stage, the intellect and intellector unite with the intellected to become a single object. This is what Patañjali stated regarding the knowledge that liberates the soul. §23

In the *Book of Patañjali* we are told that Nandikeśvara made many offerings to Mahādeva, and so was transported into Paradise in his bodily form. Also, that when Indra, the head, fornicated with the wife of the *brāhmaṇa* Nahuṣa, he was metamorphosed into a serpent as punishment. §28

Furthermore, the *Book of Patañjali* states that the soul, in relation to the ties of nescience that cause entanglement, is comparable to a grain of rice encased in its husk. The grain remains predisposed to sprouting and ripening as long as it is within the husk, locked in a cycle of generation and birth. But when the husk is winnowed from it, these episodes cease and it becomes ready to remain in a single state. Requital, on the other hand, is found within different types of §29 existents that the soul reincarnates in, depending on their lifespan, long or short, and whether their life experience is one of pleasure or suffering.

§30 QUESTION: What is the spirit's state when it subsists between merits and misdeeds, becoming trapped in the cage of rebirth for reward or punishment?

ANSWER: It is reincarnated depending on the ease and distress it has previously committed and perpetrated, oscillating between pain and pleasure.

§37–38 His liberation is not pre-eternal, for he was in the locus of entanglement before attaining it, only knowing through what is known. His knowledge there, acquired through diligence, resembled an illusion, and what was known by him was still veiled. In the locus of liberation, however, the veils are lifted, the covers removed, and the hindrances severed, leaving his essence in a state of knowing, not determined to inquire about anything hidden, disengaged from transient sensed objects, and united with permanent intelligibles.

§46 When the commentator of the *Book of Patañjali* wanted to determine the world's dimensions, he began by describing its lowest region, stating that the darkness there measures one *koṭi* and eighty-five *lakṣas*, or in *yojanas* 18,500,000. Above the darkness is Naraka, or the hells, measuring thirteen *koṭis* and twelve *lakṣas*, which is 131,200,000 *yojanas*. Above this is darkness, measuring one *lakṣa*, which is 100,000 *yojanas*. Above this darkness is a land called, because of its hardness, Vajra, meaning "a diamond," and also called "the cast thunderbolt," measuring 34,000 *yojanas*. Above it is Garbha, or "the middle land," measuring 60,000 *yojanas*. Above it is "the golden land," measuring 30,000 *yojanas*. Above that is "the seven lands," each of which measures 10,000 *yojanas*, totaling 70,000 *yojanas*. The highest of them is a land that has the *dvīpas* and the seas. Beyond the "Sweet Water" ocean is Lokā Loka, or "the place of no gathering," meaning "the Uncivilized and Uninhabited Land." After it comes the Land of Gold, measuring one *koṭi*, which is 10,000,000 *yojanas*. Above it is Pitṛ Loka, measuring 6,134,000 *yojanas*. The total of the seven *lokas*, referred to in their entirety as Brahmāṇḍa, measures fifteen *koṭi*, which is 150,000,000 *yojanas*. Above Brahmāṇḍa is a darkness called *tamas* measuring, as with the lowest darkness, 18,500,000 *yojanas*.

A citation from the *Book of Patañjali* that contradicts the earlier statement:[14] Bodies are the nets of spirits for procuring requital. He who reaches the stage of liberation has fulfilled his dues for past actions in his present form, and withdrawn from acquiring any more *karma* for the future. As a result, he frees himself from the net and no longer needs his present form. He moves freely within it, without being ensnared. He is therefore able to transport himself anywhere he likes and any time he wants, but not in the same way this occurs after death. Since even dense and contiguous bodies do not hinder his own form, how can his body be a hindrance to his spirit? §47

Five winds permeate bodies. Through two of these inhalation and exhalation occur. The third wind brings about the mixture of nutrients within the digestive system. The fourth wind causes the body's motion from one place to another. Through the fifth wind sensations are transported from one part of the body to another. §48

One infers from this that the first part is instrumental to the second. Furthermore, the third part, which is devotion, follows as instrumental to both. For through it God guides toward the attainment of liberation, and prepares a form to realize a cumulative graduation toward felicity. §57

Patañjali then adds a fantastical fourth part to these called *rasāyana*, consisting of drug treatments through which, as with alchemy, the impossible is accomplished.

§63 QUESTION: If a person has acquired *karma*, necessitating requital, while in a form that is not the one in which the acquiring of *karma* had taken place, does the long period of time between the two conditions result in the matter being forgotten?

ANSWER: Praxis accompanies the spirit because it acquires it and the body is its instrument. There is no forgetfulness with matters relating to the soul because it lies outside time and it is time that determines what is recent and distant in terms of duration. By accompanying the spirit, praxis shapes its nature and innate disposition so as to resemble that state to which it transitions. For the soul in its purity knows this, remembers it, and does not forget it. What veils the soul's light is the body's turbidity when it combines with it, as a person might remember something he knew but subsequently forget in a moment of madness, or affliction, or intoxication overcoming his mind.

§64 Do you not see that juveniles and children are happy when long life is invoked for them and are saddened when a hasty end is invoked? What meaning would these two invocations have for them had they not savored the sweetness of life and experienced the bitterness of death in previous cycles in which they had transmigrated for reasons related to requital?

§78 THIS IS THE REASON WHY THE RENUNCIANT AT THE END OF THE BOOK OF PATAÑJALI ASKED: How is liberation brought about?

ANSWER: You might say that liberation is the suspension of the three forces, returning to the source from which they emerged. You might also say that it is the return of the soul in a state of knowing to its nature.

§79 I can only compare the contents of their books on mathematics and astronomy to mother-of-pearl jumbled up with potsherds, or pearls mixed with dung, or rock crystals and pebbles gathered together.[15]

Notes

1 Heading added.

2 Heading added.

3 Reflecting Sutra I.48: "In this state of utmost lucidity, insight is truth-bearing."

4 Echoing the description of the intellect or buddhi in its most subtle form of *sattva*. For the Sanskrit yogic term *sattva* (lightness), see *three primary forces* in the Glossary.

5 The edge of the manuscript is damaged here.

6 Probably the appropriation of a Sufi term, but used here to describe the state of human conflict and sorrow that Yoga seeks to remove, as commentaries on Sutra II.16 explain.

7 Reflecting the Sanskrit *sthiti* in Sutra II.18, meaning "steadiness"; here: "inertia."

8 There is a lacuna in the manuscript due to damage that is beyond restoration.

9 Reflecting the Sanskrit term *jñātṛtvaṃ* in Sutra III.39, lit. "knowingness," and in this sutra understood as "omniscience."

10 This figure may be a reference to the commentary al-Bīrūnī states he is using at the outset in §0.5, implied by him there as being voluminous.

11 Heading added.

12 The numbering corresponds to the questions in *Kitāb Bātanjali*.

13 From the *Book of Sānk*, a lost work referred to by al-Bīrūnī in his *Hind*.

14 From the lost *Book of Sānk*.

15 A variant of this line is found in the Epilogue of *Kitāb Bātanjali*.

Glossary

abhiniveśa (Skt.) see *ties.*

abhyāsa (Skt.) see *practice.*

acquiring karma (Ar. kasb/iktisāb) the term *karma* (*karman* in Sanskrit) has a number of possible meanings, including volitional activity, the resulting deposit of such action, and its fruition. The Arabic *iktisāb* seems to reflect the second and third of these possible meanings.

action (Ar. fiʿl) probably translating *karman* (Skt.) in the sense of "volitional activity."

ʿadāwāt (Ar.) see *antipathy.*

afflictions (Ar. athqāl) reflecting the Sanskrit term *kleśa* or "cause of affliction," of which there are five, as the basic motivation forces that underlie all human activity.

ajñāna (Skt.) see *nescience.*

ʿalāʾiq (Ar.) see *ties.*

ʿālim (Ar.) see *knower.*

ʿamal (Ar.) see *praxis.*

ānanda (Skt.) see *eternal bliss.*

Andhra (Ar. al-Adharī) region on India's southeastern coast. See Map.

angelic beings (Ar. malāʾikah) referring to the *deva* (Skt.) or "angelic beings, deities," whose tempting invitations the *yogin* is warned against by Patañjali in Chapter Three.

antipathy (Ar. ʿadāwāt) a translation of Sansrit *dveṣa* or "aversion," which, along with attraction, characterizes an individual's two general modes of relationship with their environment.

anumāna (Skt.) see *received knowledge.*

apariṇāmitva (Skt.) see *immutability.*

'aql (Ar.) see *intellect.*

aṣṭāṅga yoga (Skt.) see *eight limbs.*

athqāl (Ar.) see *afflictions.*

avidyā (Skt.) see *nescience.*

bandha (Skt.) see *bondage.*

Bātanjali (Ar.) see *Patañjali.*

bharata-kumāra (Skt.) (Ar. *baratakumāra*) a class of demigod.

bhūmi (Skt.) see *level; stage.*

bhūta (Skt.) see *matter or substance.*

bondage (Ar. *withāq*) reflecting the Sanskrit *bandha* or "bondage," which is the cause of attachment of consciousness to the body, the result of fundamental misconception or error.

Brahma (Skt.) (Ar. Brāhma) the creator god in Hinduism.

brāhmaṇas (Skt.) (Ar. *barāhima*) brahmins, one of the four classes in Vedic society.

buddhi (Skt.) see *intellect.*

citta (Skt.) see *mind.*

class (Ar. *jins*) reflecting Sanskrit *jāti* in its sense of "category of existence, genus," found in a number of sutras.

concentration (Ar. *iqrār*) a translation of Sanskrit *samādhi* or "right concentration," which is defined as a state where one's thoughts diminish and one becomes like a clear jewel through the unification of consciousness and the resulting state of union with the perceived object.

desire (Ar. *raghbah*) reflecting the Sanskrit term *rāga* with its sense of "attachment" to pleasant experiences or that which accrues from objects of attraction influencing the mind.

deva (Skt.) see *angelic beings.*

devotion (Ar. *'ibādah*) a translation of Sanskrit *praṇidhāna* or "devotion," designating "devotion to the Lord" (Skt. *Īśvarapraṇidhāna*), which appears to be an alternative path to achieving liberation.

dhāt (Ar.) see *essence.*

direct observation (Ar. *'iyān*) translating Sanskrit *dṛśi* or "seeing, power of seeing." Through clear seeing, the purpose of Yoga is attained, and the *yogin* is thereby able to gain full and immediate access to the world, unencumbered by egoism.

dispassion (Ar. *zuhd*) a translation of Sanskrit *vairāgya* or "dispassion," meaning a transcendent yogic nonattachment extending both to objects in this world and the rewards of the next.

draṣṭṛ (Skt.) see *knower.*

dṛśi (Skt.) see *direct observation.*

dṛśya (Skt.) see *known objects.*

dveṣa (Skt.) see *antipathy.*

dvīpa (Skt.) (Ar. *dība*) an island or continent in Hindu cosmology.

eight limbs (Ar. *thamānī khiṣāl*) a reference to Sanskrit *aṣṭāṅga yoga* or the "Yoga of eight members," containing the eight limbs of Yoga, each of which may be considered as a distinct form of practice: restraint (Skt. *yama*), observance (Skt. *niyama*), postures (Skt. *āsana*), control of breath (Skt. *prāṇāyāma*), sense withdrawal (Skt. *pratyāhāra*), concentration (Skt. *dhāraṇā*), meditation (Skt. *dhyāna*), and right concentration (Skt. *samādhi*).

ekatva (Skt.) see *unification.*

entanglement (Ar. *irtibāk*) seems to reflect Sanskrit *saṃ yoga* or "confusion"—namely, the mistaken linking of *puruṣa* (seer/higher self) with *prakṛti* (manifest realm).

essence (Ar. *dhāt*) a translation of Sanskrit *puruṣa*, which has the sense of the "seer or higher self," rather than simply "self" in its more basic meaning. It is experienced as the highest reality, and therefore is the supreme value.

eternal bliss (Ar. *al-saʿādah al-abadiyyah*) a possible translation of Sanskrit *ānanda*, meaning "bliss" or "joy" as a state of cognitive samādhi.

exerting the body (Ar. *itʿāb al-badan*) a translation of Sanskrit *tapas* or "ascesis," comprising all those exercises that fall outside the categories of self-study (Skt. *svādhyāya*) and devotion (Skt. *praṇidhāna*).

fiʿl (Ar.) see *action.*

form (Ar. *qālib*) a translation of Sanskrit *rūpa*, meaning "form, shape, figure, outward appearance."

Ganga (Skt.) (Ar. Kanka) the Ganges River. See Map.

generation (Ar. *tawallud*) probably Sanskrit *saṃsāra*, meaning "rebirth" or "cycle of existence," referring to being enmeshed in the world of change with unending rounds of rebirth, and nescience of one's true identity. The term does not actually appear in the *Yoga Sutras* of Patañjali.

guṇas (Skt.) see *three primary forces.*

Hiraṇyagarbha (Skt.) (Ar. Hīrannakarba) name of Brahma (as born from a golden egg).

ḥulūl (Ar.) see *incarnation.*

ʿibādah (Ar.) see *devotion.*

ʿilm (Ar.) see *knowledge.*

immutability (Ar. *taʾabbud*) translating Sanskrit *apariṇāmitva*, "immutability," a status only *puruṣa* (seer; higher self) is able to enjoy. Its authentic immortal identity is never lost in spite of all the modifications of the mind and changes in the world.

incarnation (Ar. *ḥulūl*) a translation of Sanskrit *jāti*, meaning "birth, production, position assigned by caste or rank." In other contexts it also denotes "genus."

Indra a Vedic deity in Hinduism.

intaqala (Ar.) see *transition/transported.*

intellect (Ar. *ʿaql*) reflecting the Sanskrit term *buddhi* or "intellect, cognition," which is the faculty of intelligence and discernment in a sentient entity, and the highest power in the process of sensation.

intelligibles (Ar. *maʿqūlāt*) reflecting the Sanskrit term *pratyaya* or "presented idea"—namely, the perceptions of the empirical consciousness.

iqrār (Ar.) see *concentration.*

irtibāk (Ar.) see *entanglement.*

irtiyāḍ (Ar.) see *meditational praxis.*

īśvara (Skt.) an idealized deity defined as the perfect soul untouched by afflictions, actions, fruitions, or their residue.

itʿāb al-badan (Ar.) see *exerting the body.*

ittiḥād (Ar.) see *unification.*

ʿiyān (Ar.) see *direct observation.*

jahl (Ar.) see *nescience.*

Jambu Dvīpa (Skt.) (Ar. Janbu Dība) one of the Purāṇically famous Saptadvīpas (seven continents). These seven continents are embankments separating the seven seas. Jambu Dvīpa, Krauñca Dvīpa, Śāka Dvīpa, and Puṣkara Dvīpa are included in the seven islands.

jāti (Skt.) see *class; incarnation; qualification.*

jazā' (Ar.) see *recompense.*

jins (Ar.) see *class.*

jñāna (Skt.) see *knowledge.*

kaivalya (Skt.) see *liberation.*

Kanauj (Ar. Kannawj) city in northern India on the Ganges River. See Map.

Kapila (Ar. Kabila) a renowned ancient sage.

karma (variant of Skt. *karman*) see *acquiring karma; action; praxis.*

kasb/iktisāb (Ar.) see *acquiring karma.*

kayfiyyah (Ar.) see *qualification.*

khabar (Ar.) see *received knowledge.*

khalāṣ (Ar.) see *liberation.*

kleśa (Skt.) see *afflictions.*

knower (Ar. *'ālim*) a rendition of Sanskrit *draṣṭṛ* or "seer," characterizing the Self (Skt. *puruṣa*) or the power of awareness, whereas the world, in its unmanifest and manifest form, is that which is seen by the seer.

knowledge (Ar. *'ilm*) translating Sanskrit *jñāna* or discriminative "knowledge" that arises from Yoga and leads to liberation. The same term is also used to render Sanskrit *saṃbodhaḥ* or "knowledge, understanding."

known objects (Ar. *ma'lūmāt*) a rendition of Sanskrit *dṛśya* or "seen," consisting of the entire body of the world or nature (Skt. *prakṛti*), including its causal core.

koṭi (Skt.) (Ar. *kūrtī*) ten million.

kriyā (Skt.) see *praxis.*

Kshatriya (Skt. *kṣatriya*, Ar. *kshatra*) one of the four classes in Vedic society.

lābhaḥ (Skt.) see *recompense.*

lakṣa (Skt.) (Ar. *laksha*) one hundred thousand.

level (Ar. *ṭabaqah*) echoing the Sanskrit term *bhūmi*, meaning "stage, position, place, ground."

liberation (Ar. *khalāṣ*) reflecting Sanskrit *kaivalya*, meaning a liberated state of "perfect aloneness" or "final liberation," which consists in the full realization of the Self (Skt. *puruṣa*) or the freedom of pure identity as Self, giving rise to discriminative discernment and the cessation of afflicted action.

loka (Skt.) (Ar. *lūka*) the universe or any division of it in the cosmography of Hinduism.

māddah (Ar.) see *matter or substance.*

Mahādeva (Skt.) (Ar. Mahādīwa) a name of Shiva, one of the three main gods in Hinduism.

mahāvideha (Skt.) (Ar. *mahābidaha*) an external non-imaginary fluctuation of consciousness in the Yoga system of philosophy.

maḥsūsāt (Ar.) see *sensed objects.*

malā'ikah (Ar.) see *angelic beings.*

ma'lūmāt (Ar.) see *known objects.*

ma'qūlāt (Ar.) see *intelligibles.*

ma'rifah (Ar.) see *understanding.*

martabah (Ar.) see *stage.*

matter/substance (Ar. *māddah*) sometimes, though not exclusively, translating Sanskrit *bhūta* or "elements," referring to earth, water, fire, air, and space. The Sanskrit term can also indicate a "constituent of the manifest world."

meditational praxis (Ar. *irtiyāḍ*) possibly attempting to reflect Sanskrit *pratiprasava* or "subtilization," which carries the sense of a (mental) process bringing about an inverse movement, and a return to the original state, or a reabsorption into the transcendent purity of being itself.

mind (Ar. *qalb*) reflecting the Sanskrit term *citta* or "mind, mind stuff, consciousness," which is central to the Yoga system and may be described as a vehicle for perception that presents the contents of experience to the Self.

Mount Meru (Ar. Jabal Mīrū) the sacred five-peaked mountain of Hindu cosmology.

mukāfa'ah (Ar.) see *requital.*

mūla (Skt.) see *web.*

nafs (Ar.) see *soul.*

Nahuṣa (Skt.) (Ar. Nahusha) a king of the Aila Dynasty in Hindu mythology.

Nandikeśvara (Skt.) (Ar. Nandikīshfara) name of one of Shiva's chief attendants.

Naraka (Skt.) infernal/hellish realms or states of existence.

nescience (Ar. *jahl*) covering both Sanskrit *avidyā* and *ajñāna*, referring to the *yogin*'s root affliction with its various forms of karmic bondage, the result of spiritual nescience of authentic identity, being the Self (Skt. *puruṣa*) that would lead to spiritual freedom.

pariṇāma (Skt.) see *transition/transported.*

Patañjali (Ar. Bātanjali) fourth/fifth century AD author of the Sanskrit *Yoga Sutras.*

phala (Skt.) see *requital.*

practice (Ar. *ta'wīd*) a translation of Sanskrit *abhyāsa* or the "application of practice, repeated exercise, discipline, study," referring to the various practices described in Patañjali's first chapter.

prajñā (Skt.) see *understanding.*

praṇidhāna (Skt.) see *devotion.*

pratiprasava (Skt.) see *meditational praxis.*

pratyaya (Skt.) see *intelligibles.*

praxis (Ar. *'amal*) covering both Sanskrit *karman* (see also *acquiring karma* and *action*) and *kriyā* or "doing, performing, work, action"; and referring, furthermore, to *kriyā yoga*, which involves austerity, self-study, and dedication to *īśvara* with the express purpose of uprooting the influence of impurity (Skt. *kleśa*).

puruṣa (Skt.) see *essence; soul; spirit.*

qalb (Ar.) see *mind.*

qālib (Ar.) see *form.*

al-qiwā al-thalāth al-ūlā (Ar.) see *three primary forces.*

qualification (Ar. *kayfiyyah*) sometimes reflecting the Sanskrit term *jāti* in its sense of "category, life state," found in a number of sutras.

rāga (Skt.) see *desire.*

raghbah (Ar.) see *desire.*

rasāyana (Skt.) a medicine preventing old age and prolonging life.

received knowledge (Ar. *khabar*) translating Sanskrit *anumāna* or "inference," with the particular sense of insight gained from tradition. Ordinary knowledge, derived from tradition (testimony) or inference (Skt. *anumāna*), is said to deal only with the "general," whereas the "particular" is the proper domain of perception.

recompense (Ar. *jazā'*) translating Sanskrit *lābhaḥ* in a number of sutras, meaning "obtained, gotten, gained."

reincarnation (Ar. *taraddud*) echoing Sanskrit *vipāka* with the literal sense of "fruition, ripening, effect, result." Rooted in nescience, afflicted action causes repeated fruition (Skt. *vipāka*) of situations or births and lifespan, furthering samsaric experience.

requital (Ar. *mukāfa'ah*) translating Sanskrit *phala*, meaning "fruit, consequences, result," referring to the results or "fruit" of a person's actions, be they meritorious or demeritorious.

ribāṭ (Ar.) see *web.*

rūḥ (Ar.) see *spirit.*

rūḥāniyyīn (Ar.) see *spiritual beings.*

rūpa (Skt.) see *form.*

al-saʿādah al-abadiyyah (Ar.) see *eternal bliss.*

samādhi (Skt.) see *concentration.*

saṃsāra (Skt.) see *generation; transmigration.*

saṃyoga (Skt.) see *entanglement.*

sensed objects (Ar. *maḥsūsāt*) echoing Sanskrit *viṣaya*, meaning "an object of senses, sense objects."

siddhas (Skt.) (Ar. *sidda*) referring to perfected masters who have achieved a high degree of physical as well as spiritual perfection or enlightenment.

soul (Ar. *nafs*) a translation of Sanskrit *puruṣa* with its primary sense of "Self, highest self," but sometimes also translated as "soul" as in the *Kitāb Bātanjali.*

spirit (Ar. *rūḥ*) a translation of Sanskrit *puruṣa* with its primary sense of "Self, highest self" but sometimes also translated as "spirit" as in the *Kitāb Bātanjali.*

spiritual beings (Ar. *rūḥāniyyīn*) a translation of Sanskrit *videha*, meaning "discarnate, bodiless, incorporeal" *yogins*, who incorrectly consider the enhanced sense of well-being in eternal bliss (Skt. *ānanda*) to be the supreme attainment in Yoga, and consequently have not yet achieved liberation.

stage (Ar. *martabah*) translating Sanskrit *bhūmi*, meaning "stage, level, place, ground."

ta'abbud (Ar.) see *immutability.*

ṭabaqah (Ar.) see *level.*

tamas (Skt.) (Ar. *tama*) darkness.

tanāsukh (Ar.) see *transmigration.*

tapas (Skt.) see *exerting the body.*

taraddud (Ar.) see *reincarnation.*

tawallud (Ar.) see *generation.*

ta'wīd (Ar.) see *practice.*

thamānī khiṣāl (Ar.) see *eight limbs.*

three primary forces (Ar. *al-qiwā al-thalāth al-uwal*) referring to the three *guṇas* (Skt.) or "primary constituents," the basic strands or qualities of Sanskrit *prakṛti* (matter), consisting of *tamas* (darkness), *rajas* (activity), and *sattva* (lightness).

ties (Ar. *'alā'iq*) a translation of Sanskrit *abhiniveśa*, meaning "clinging to life, tenacity, desire for continuity, will to live," referring to the insatiable desire to hold on to life even among the wise and inextricably linked to *karma.*

transition/transported (Ar. *intaqala*) echoing Sanskrit *pariṇāma*, meaning "transformation, change, alteration, evolution, development, ripeness, result."

transmigration (Ar. *tanāsukh*) referring to Sanskrit *saṃsāra*, meaning "transmigration, rebirth, cycle," being a blind repetition of prior action, through unending rounds of rebirth and ignorance of one's true identity.

understanding (Ar. *ma'rifah*) a translation of Sanskrit *prajñā*, meaning "wisdom, knowledge, intelligence, insight," disclosed within the deeper levels of the mind, which progressively leads to a clearer understanding and realization of one's intrinsic identity as Self.

unification (Ar. *ittiḥād*) translating both Sanskrit *ekatva*, meaning "oneness, uniformity," and *sāmya*, meaning "sameness, singleness."

vairāgya (Skt.) see *dispassion.*

Vajra (Skt.) (Ar. Bazra) diamond or thunderbolt.

Veda (Skt.) (Ar. Bītha) the Hindu scriptures.

videha (Skt.) see *spiritual beings.*

vipāka (Skt.) see *reincarnation.*

viṣaya (Skt.) see *sensed objects.*

Vishvadhara (Skt.) (Ar. Bisa Wazadarwā) an abode of the universe; a son of Medhatithi (*Bhāgavata Purāṇa*); another name for Vishnu.

web (Ar. *ribāṭ*) translating Sanskrit *mūla*, meaning "root, foundation," referring to the five afflictions that are the root of the residue of *karma*. The commentators refer to these afflictions as "binders" (Skt. *bandhaka*) that *catch* and *bind* a creature.

withāq (Ar.) see *bondage.*

yojana (Skt.) (Ar. *jawzana*) a unit of distance, probably between five and ten kilometers.

zuhd (Ar.) see *dispassion.*

Table of Correspondences

In corresponding sequential order as they occur in each question or answer.

KITĀB BĀTANJALI	YOGA SUTRAS OF *PATAÑJALI*
§2.1	I. 2
§3.2	I. 3
§4.2	I. 4
§5.2–6	I. 5 / I. 7 / I. 8 / I. 9 / I. 10 / I. 11
§6.2–3	I. 12 / I. 13 / I. 14 / I. 15 / I. 16
§7.2	I. 17 / I. 18
§8.2	I. 19 / I. 20
§10.1	I. 22
§10.2	I. 21
§11.2	I. 23
§12.2	I. 24 / I. 25
§13.2	I. 26
§14.2	I. 25
§15.2	I. 27
§16.2	I. 26
§18.2	I. 28 / I. 29
§19.1	I. 29
§19.2	I. 30
§20.2	I. 31
§21.2	I. 32
§22.2	I. 33 / I. 34

KITĀB BĀTANJALI	YOGA SUTRAS OF *PATAÑJALI*
§23.2–3	I. 40 / I. 41 / I. 46 / I. 42 / I. 49 / I. 44 / I. 45 / I. 49 / I. 48
§23.4	III.11
§24.2	II. 1
§25.2	II. 2
§26.2	II. 3 / II. 4
§27.2–7	II. 5 / II. 6 / II. 7 / II. 8 / II. 9 / II. 10
§28.1	II. 11
§28.2	II. 12
§29.2	II. 13
§30.2	II. 14
§31.2	II. 15
§32.2	II. 16
§33.2	II. 17
§34.2	II. 18
§35.2	II. 18
§36.2	II. 20 / II. 21 / II. 23
§37.1	II. 22
§38.2	II. 24 / II. 26 / II. 25
§39.2	II. 27
§40.2	II. 28
§41.2–11	II. 29 / II. 30 / II. 31 / II. 34 / II. 33 / II. 35 / II. 36 / II. 37 / II. 38 / II. 39 / II. 40 / II. 43 / II. 42 / II. 44 / II. 45 / II. 46 / II. 47 / II. 48 / II. 49 / II. 50 / II. 51 / II. 52 / II. 53 / II. 54 / II. 55 / III. 1 / III. 2 / III. 3 / III. 4 / III. 5 / III. 6 / III. 7 / III. 8
§42.2	III. 9 / III. 10 / III. 11
§43.2	III. 16
§44.2	III. 12 / III. 15 / III. 14 / III. 13
§45.2	III. 17 / III. 18 / III. 19 / III. 20
§46.2–8	III. 21 / III. 22 / III. 23 / III. 24 / III. 25 / III. 26
§46.16–24	III. 27 / III. 28 / III. 29 / III. 30 / III. 31 / III. 32 / III. 34 / III. 35 / III. 36

KITĀB BĀTANJALI	YOGA SUTRAS OF *PATAÑJALI*
§47.2	III. 37 / III. 38
§48.2–6	III. 39 / III. 40 / III. 41 / III. 42
§49.2–3	III. 43 / III. 44 / III. 45 / III. 46
§50.2	III. 47 / III. 48 / III. 49
§51.2	III. 50 / III. 51
§53.2	III. 52
§54.2	III. 53
§55.2	III. 54
§56.2	III. 55
§57.2	IV. 1
§58.2	IV. 2
§59.2	IV. 3
§60.1	IV. 4
§60.2	IV. 5
§61.2	IV. 6
§62.2	IV. 8 / IV. 7
§63.2	IV. 9
§65.1	IV. 10
§65.2	IV. 11
§66.2	IV. 12 / IV. 13
§67.2	IV. 14
§68.2	IV. 15 / IV. 16 / IV. 17
§69.2	IV. 19
§70.2	IV. 20–24
§71.2	IV. 25
§72.2	IV. 26
§73.2	IV. 27
§74.2	IV. 28 / IV. 29 / IV. 30 / IV. 31
§75.1	IV. 32
§75.2	IV. 33
§78.2	IV. 34

Bibliography

Works by al-Bīrūnī

Al-Āthār l-bāqiyah ʿan al-qurūn al-khāliyah. Edited by Eduard Sachau. Leipzig: Brockhaus, 1878. Reprint Leipzig: Otto Harrassowitz, 1923.

"Al-Bīrūnī's Übersetzung des Yoga-Sūtra des Patañjali." Edited by Helmut Ritter. Oriens 9, no. 2 (Dec. 31, 1956): 165–200.

Kitāb Taḥdīd nihāyāt al-amākin li-taṣḥīḥ masāfāt al-masākin. Edited by Pavel Georgievič Bulgakov. Cairo: Maṭbaʿat Lajnat al-Taʾlīf wa-l-Tarjamah wa-l-Nashr, 1962.

Kitāb Taḥqīq mā li-l-Hind min maqūlah maqbūlah fi-l-ʿaql aw mardhūlah. Edited by Eduard Sachau. London: Trübner, 1887. Reprint, Hyderabad: Maṭbaʿat Majlis Dāʾirat al-Maʿārif al-ʿUthmāniyyah, 1958.

Al-Qānūn al-Masʿūdī fī-l-hayʾah wa-l-nujūm. Edited by Syed Hasan Barani. Hyderabad: Maṭbaʿat Majlis Dāʾirat al-Maʿārif al-ʿUthmāniyyah, 1954–56.

Al-Bīrūnī and Ibn Sīnā. *Al-Asʾilah wa-l-ajwibah.* Edited by Seyyed Hossein Nasr and Mahdi Mohaghegh. Tehran: High Council of Culture and Art, 1973.

Secondary Sources

Akasoy, Anna. "Philosophical Correspondence." In *EI3*.

Boilot, D. J. "Bīrūnī." In *EI2*.

Bosworth, C. E. "Bīrūnī: Life." In *EIran*.

Chapple, Christopher Key. *Yoga and the Luminous: Patañjali's Spiritual Path to Freedom.* Albany: State University of New York Press, 2008.

Dasgupta, Surendranath. *Yoga Philosophy in Relation to Other Systems of Indian Thought*. Calcutta: University of Calcutta, 1930.

Daiber, H. "Masā'il wa-Adjwiba." In *EI2*.

Feuerstein, Georg. *The Yoga-Sūtra of Patañjali: A New Translation and Commentary*. Rochester, Vermont: Inner Traditions, 1989.

Flood, Gavin. *An Introduction to Hinduism*. Cambridge: Cambridge University Press, 1996.

Gallop, David. *Phaedo*. Oxford: Oxford University Press, 2009.

Goichon, Anne-Marie. *Lexique de la langue philosophique d'Ibn Sīnā*. Paris: Desclée de Brouwer, 1938.

Hansbury, Mary. *John the Solitary on the Soul*. Piscataway: Gorgias Press, 2013.

Kozah, Mario. *The Birth of Indology as an Islamic Science: Al-Bīrūnī's Treatise on Yoga Psychology*. Leiden: Brill, 2015.

Pines, Shlomo, and Tuvia Gelblum, "Al-Bīrūnī's Arabic Version of Patañjali's Yogasūtra." *Bulletin of the School of Oriental and African Studies* 29, no. 2, (1966): 302–25; 40, no. 3, (1977): 522–49; 46, no. 2, (1983): 258–304; 52, no. 2, (1989): 265–305.

Rosenthal, Franz, "On Some Epistemological and Methodological Presuppositions of al-Bīrūnī." In *Beyrunî'ye Armağan*, edited by A. Sayili, 145–67. Ankara: Türk tarih kurumu basimevi, 1974.

Whicher, Ian. *The Integrity of the Yoga Darśana*. Albany: State University of New York Press, 1998.

Further Reading

Al-Bīrūnī. *Alberuni's India: An Account of the Religion, Philosophy, Literature, Chronology, Astronomy, Customs, Laws, and Astrology of India*. Translated and edited by E. Sachau. Arabic in 1 vol. London: Trübner, 1887. English in 2 vols. London: Trübner, 1888.

Feuerstein, Georg. *The Yoga-Sūtra of Patañjali: A New Translation and Commentary*. Rochester, Vermont: Inner Traditions, 1989.

Kozah, Mario. *The Birth of Indology as an Islamic Science. Al-Bīrūnī's Treatise on Yoga Psychology*. Leiden: Brill, 2015.

Waardenburg, Jacques. *Muslim Perceptions of Other Religions: A Historical Survey*. New York: Oxford University Press, 1999.

Whicher, Ian. *The Integrity of the Yoga Darśana*. New York: State University of New York Press, 1998.

Wink, André. *Al-Hind, the Making of the Indo-Islamic World*. Vol. 2. Leiden: Brill, 1991.

Yarshater, Ehsan, ed. *Biruni Symposium*. New York: Columbia University, Iran Center, 1976.

Index

Paradise, §28.2, §46.5, §51.2, §52.2; Appendix: §28
particulars, §23.3, §49.3
past, xxxiii, §13.2, §16.2, §41.2, §43.2, §45.2, §47.2, §65.2, §§66.1–2; Appendix: §16, §47
Patañjali, xiii–xvii, xxx–xxxi, xxxvi–xxxviii, §§1.1–2, §46.16; Appendix: §23, §57; *Book of*, xiii, xxix–xxx, xxxiv–xxxv, xxxviii, xlivn30, §23.4, §79.1, §79.6; Appendix: §1, §2, §12, §21, §28, §29, §46, §47, §78
perception, xxxiii, §0.7, §1.1, §34.2, §50.2, §57.1, §70.2
Peripatetic, xxvii–xxviii, xxxiii
Persia, xxv
Phaedo, xxxi, xxxvi
philosophy, xi, xiii–xvii, xxvi–xxix, xxxi–xxxii, xxxvi–xxxix, xlii, §0.3
Pitṛ Loka, §46.12; Appendix: §46
place, §14.2, §41.2, §46.12, §46.24; Appendix: §14, §46
Plato, xxxi, xxxvi
powers, §1.2, §2.1, §4.2, §5.1, §6.1, §6.2, §27.1, 28.1, §29.2
practice, xv–xvi, xxn21, xxx, §6.2, §11.1, §18.2, §24.2, §42.2, §43.1, §57.2, §74.2, §79.2, §79.4; Appendix: §1
practitioner, xxxvi, §24.2, §74.2
praxis, xxxii, §1.2, §6.2, §11.2, §19.2, §35.2, §46.4, §47.2, §48.1, §57.1, §63.2, §74.2; Appendix: §63
present, xxxiii, §13.2, §41.2, §43.2, §46.7, §47.2, §53.2, §65.2, §66.2, §68.2; Appendix: §47
psychological, xxx, xxxiv, xxxvi–xxxix, xlii
purification, xxxiii, §0.4, §41.3, §50.2, §56.2, §67.2, §73.1, §74.2
Pythagorean-Hermetic, xxviii

qalb. *See* mind (heart)
qālib. *See* form
Qānūn (*Masʿūd's Canonical Rules on the Shape of the Universe and the Stars*), xxv
qiwā al-thalāth al-ūlā. *See* forces; three primary forces
qualification, §34.2, §§55.1–2
Questions and Answers, xxvii–xxviii

rasāyana, §57.2; Appendix: §57
reality, §5.3, §5.5, §27.2, §45.2, §46.24, §50.2
received knowledge, §5.2
recompense, xxxiii, §24.2, §28.2, §47.2, §56.3, §62.2, §§65.1–2; recompensed, §41.2, §§43.1–2, §45.1, §46.7–8, §46.14
reincarnation, xxxviii, §29.2
renunciant (*yogin*), xxxvi, §0.3, §1.1, §26.2, §46.9, §46.23, §47.2, §§48.4–6, §§49.1–3, §50.2, §§51.1–2, §57.1, §58.1, §60.1, §62.2, §65.2; Appendix: §12, §78
renunciation, §§57.1–2, §61.1, §62.1
requital, §12.2, §28.2, §§29.1–2, §31.2, §41.2, §46.2, §47.1, §56.3, §62.2, §64.2, §66.2; Appendix: §12, §29, §47, §63, §64
reward, §24.2, §30.1, §41.2, §46.2, §59.1, §62.2, §65.2, §74.2; Appendix: §30
Ritter, Helmut, xxix
Rosenthal, Franz, xxx

salvation, xvi, xxxvi–xxxvii, §0.7
Sāṃkhya, xiii–xiv, xxxiii
Sanskrit, xii, xv–xvi, xxix, xxxv, xxxvii–xxxix, xli–xlii, §46.13, 57n4, 57n7, 57n9
Sapta Pātāla, §46.10
seeds, §26.2, §27.7
seen, §23.2, §68.2
seer, §68.2
self-realization, xxxii
sense perception, xxxiii, §1.1, §34.2, §57.1
sensed objects, §46.24; Appendix: §37–38
Shams al-Maʿālī Qābūs ibn Wushmagīr, xxviii
siddhas, §46.23
sin(s), §0.3, §39.2, §59.1, §62.2, §65.2, §74.2
śisyas (disciples), xxx
snake, §41.2
soul (*puruṣa*), xiii, xxxii–xxxviii, §0.4, §§0.6–7, §1.2, §§2.1–2, §§4.1–2, §5.1, §§6.1–2, §18.2, §§19.1–2, §§20.1–2, §22.2, §23.2, §25.2, §27.2, §27.5, §28.2, §29.2, §30.1, §§31.1–2, §39.2, §§41.2–3, §41.11, §46.4, §46.6, §46.24, §47.2, §50.2, §51.2, §56.2, §59.2, §63.2, §67.2, §78.2, §79.2; Appendix: §18, §22, §23, §29, §63, §78
sound, §0.7, §46.5, §48.5
species, §47.2, §48.4, §55.2
spirit, xxxvii, §5.4, §47.2; Appendix: §47, §63
spiritual ascesis, xxxii
spiritual being(s), §0.6, §8.1, §9.2, §41.3, §58.1
stage(s), xxxii–xxxiii, §0.2, §6.3, §10.2, §23.1, §23.3, §§24.1–2, §41.9, §41.11, §42.2, §§51.1–2, §74.2; Appendix: §23, §47
stars, §§46.16–17
station, §32.2
substance, §39.2, §44.2, §§46.19–20, §56.2. *See also* matter
suffering, xvi, §29.2, §39.2, §41.2, §41.4, §52.2, §79.2; Appendix: §29
Sufi, xxxi, §0.4, 57n6
sun, §4.1, §5.3, §27.3, §46.8, §46.14
sutra, xxxi, xxxv, xlii, 57n3, 57n6, 57n7, 57n9
Suvarṇa, §46.10
Syriac, xxxvi

Ṭabaristān, xxviii, xliiin7
tamas, §46.12; Appendix: §46
three primary forces, §50.2, §58.2, §66.2, §67.1, §75.1, §78.2, 57n4. *See also* forces
ties, §2.2, §26.2, §27.6, §41.11; Appendix: §29
time, §13.2, §16.2, §23.3, §41.2, §44.2, §53.2, §§63.1–2, §65.2, §66.2, §68.2, §§75.1–2; Appendix: §2, §16, §47, §63
tortoise, §46.22, §48.4; Appendix: §2
transcendence, xxxiii
transformation, xxxiii
transition, §42.2, §63.2, §66.2, §77.2; Appendix: §63. *See also* transported
translation, xi–xvi, xxvii–xxx, xxxiv–xxxviii, xli–xlii, §0.5, §79.1
transmigration, xxxii, xxxviii, §0.4
Transoxania, xxv

About the NYU Abu Dhabi Institute

The Library of Arabic Literature is supported by a grant from the NYU Abu Dhabi Institute, a major hub of intellectual and creative activity and advanced research. The Institute hosts academic conferences, workshops, lectures, film series, performances, and other public programs directed both to audiences within the UAE and to the worldwide academic and research community. It is a center of the scholarly community for Abu Dhabi, bringing together faculty and researchers from institutions of higher learning throughout the region.

NYU Abu Dhabi, through the NYU Abu Dhabi Institute, is a world-class center of cutting-edge research, scholarship, and cultural activity. The Institute creates singular opportunities for leading researchers from across the arts, humanities, social sciences, sciences, engineering, and the professions to carry out creative scholarship and conduct research on issues of major disciplinary, multidisciplinary, and global significance.

About the Translator

Mario Kozah B.A. Hons., M.A., Ph.D. (Oriental Studies, University of Cambridge) is Assistant Professor of Islamic History and Civilization at the Department of Humanities in the College of Arts and Sciences, Qatar University. His publications include a monograph on al-Bīrūnī titled *The Birth of Indology as an Islamic Science: Al-Bīrūnī's Treatise on Yoga Psychology* (Leiden: Brill, 2015).

The Library of Arabic Literature

For more details on individual titles, visit www.libraryofarabicliterature.org

Classical Arabic Literature: A Library of Arabic Literature Anthology
Selected and translated by Geert Jan van Gelder (2012)

A Treasury of Virtues: Sayings, Sermons, and Teachings of ʿAlī, by al-Qāḍī al-Quḍāʿī, with the *One Hundred Proverbs* attributed to al-Jāḥiẓ
Edited and translated by Tahera Qutbuddin (2013)

The Epistle on Legal Theory, by al-Shāfiʿī
Edited and translated by Joseph E. Lowry (2013)

Leg over Leg, by Aḥmad Fāris al-Shidyāq
Edited and translated by Humphrey Davies (4 volumes; 2013–14)

Virtues of the Imām Aḥmad ibn Ḥanbal, by Ibn al-Jawzī
Edited and translated by Michael Cooperson (2 volumes; 2013–15)

The Epistle of Forgiveness, by Abū l-ʿAlāʾ al-Maʿarrī
Edited and translated by Geert Jan van Gelder and Gregor Schoeler (2 volumes; 2013–14)

The Principles of Sufism, by ʿĀʾishah al-Bāʿūniyyah
Edited and translated by Th. Emil Homerin (2014)

The Expeditions: An Early Biography of Muḥammad, by Maʿmar ibn Rāshid
Edited and translated by Sean W. Anthony (2014)

Two Arabic Travel Books

Accounts of China and India, by Abū Zayd al-Sīrāfī

Edited and translated by Tim Mackintosh-Smith (2014)

Mission to the Volga, by Aḥmad ibn Faḍlān

Edited and translated by James Montgomery (2014)

Disagreements of the Jurists: A Manual of Islamic Legal Theory, by al-Qāḍī al-Nuʿmān

Edited and translated by Devin J. Stewart (2015)

Consorts of the Caliphs: Women and the Court of Baghdad, by Ibn al-Sāʿī

Edited by Shawkat M. Toorawa and translated by the Editors of the Library of Arabic Literature (2015)

What ʿĪsā ibn Hishām Told Us, by Muḥammad al-Muwayliḥī

Edited and translated by Roger Allen (2 volumes; 2015)

The Life and Times of Abū Tammām, by Abū Bakr Muḥammad ibn Yaḥyā al-Ṣūlī

Edited and translated by Beatrice Gruendler (2015)

The Sword of Ambition: Bureaucratic Rivalry in Medieval Egypt, by ʿUthmān ibn Ibrāhīm al-Nābulusī

Edited and translated by Luke Yarbrough (2016)

Brains Confounded by the Ode of Abū Shādūf Expounded, by Yūsuf al-Shirbīnī

Edited and translated by Humphrey Davies (2 volumes; 2016)

Light in the Heavens: Sayings of the Prophet Muḥammad, by al-Qāḍī al-Quḍāʿī

Edited and translated by Tahera Qutbuddin (2016)

Risible Rhymes, by Muḥammad ibn Maḥfūẓ al-Sanhūrī

Edited and translated by Humphrey Davies (2016)

A Hundred and One Nights

Edited and translated by Bruce Fudge (2016)

The Excellence of the Arabs, by Ibn Qutaybah
Edited by James E. Montgomery and Peter Webb
Translated by Sarah Bowen Savant and Peter Webb (2017)

Scents and Flavors: A Syrian Cookbook
Edited and translated by Charles Perry (2017)

Arabian Satire: Poetry from 18th-Century Najd, by Ḥmēdān al-Shwēʿir
Edited and translated by Marcel Kurpershoek (2017)

In Darfur: An Account of the Sultanate and Its People, by Muḥammad ibn ʿUmar al-Tūnisī
Edited and translated by Humphrey Davies (2 volumes; 2018)

War Songs, by ʿAntarah ibn Shaddād
Edited by James E. Montgomery
Translated by James E. Montgomery with Richard Sieburth (2018)

Arabian Romantic: Poems on Bedouin Life and Love, by ʿAbdallah ibn Sbayyil
Edited and translated by Marcel Kurpershoek (2018)

Dīwān ʿAntarah ibn Shaddād: A Literary-Historical Study, by James E. Montgomery (2018)

Stories of Piety and Prayer: Deliverance Follows Adversity, by al-Muḥassin ibn ʿAlī al-Tanūkhī
Edited and translated by Julia Bray (2019)

Tajrīd sayf al-himmah li-stikhrāj mā fī dhimmat al-dhimmah: A Scholarly Edition of ʿUthmān ibn Ibrāhīm al-Nābulusī's Text, by Luke Yarbrough (2019)

The Philosopher Responds: An Intellectual Correspondence from the Tenth Century, by Abū Ḥayyān al-Tawḥīdī and Abū ʿAlī Miskawayh
Edited by Bilal Orfali and Maurice A. Pomerantz
Translated by Sophia Vasalou and James E. Montgomery (2 volumes; 2019)

The Discourses: Reflections on History, Sufism, Theology, and Literature—Volume One, by al-Ḥasan al-Yūsī
Edited and translated by Justin Stearns (2020)

Impostures, by al-Ḥarīrī
Translated by Michael Cooperson (2020)

Maqāmāt Abī Zayd al-Sarūjī, by al-Ḥarīrī
Edited by Michael Cooperson (2020)

The Yoga Sutras of Patañjali, by Abū Rayḥān al-Bīrūnī
Edited and translated by Mario Kozah (2020)

The Book of Charlatans, by Jamāl al-Dīn ʿAbd al-Raḥīm al-Jawbarī
Edited by Manuela Dengler
Translated by Humphrey Davies (2020)

A Physician on the Nile: A Description of Egypt and Journal of a Plague Year, by ʿAbd al-Laṭīf al-Baghdādī
Edited and translated by Tim Mackintosh-Smith (2021)

The Book of Travels, by Ḥannā Diyāb
Edited by Johannes Stephan
Translated by Elias Muhanna (2 volumes; 2021)

Kalīlah and Dimnah: Fables of Virtue and Vice, by Ibn al-Muqaffaʿ
Edited by Michael Fishbein
Translated by Michael Fishbein and James E. Montgomery (2021)

Love, Death, Fame: Poetry and Lore from the Emirati Oral Tradition, by al-Māyidī ibn Ẓāhir
Edited and translated by Marcel Kurpershoek (2022)

The Essence of Reality: A Defense of Philosophical Sufism, by ʿAyn al-Quḍāt
Edited and translated by Mohammed Rustom (2022)

English-only Paperbacks

Leg over Leg, by Aḥmad Fāris al-Shidyāq (2 volumes; 2015)

The Expeditions: An Early Biography of Muḥammad, by Maʿmar ibn Rāshid (2015)

The Epistle on Legal Theory: A Translation of al-Shāfiʿī's Risālah, by al-Shāfiʿī (2015)

The Epistle of Forgiveness, by Abū l-ʿAlāʾ al-Maʿarrī (2016)

The Principles of Sufism, by ʿĀʾishah al-Bāʿūniyyah (2016)

A Treasury of Virtues: Sayings, Sermons, and Teachings of ʿAlī, by al-Qāḍī al-Quḍāʿī with the *One Hundred Proverbs* attributed to al-Jāḥiẓ (2016)

The Life of Ibn Ḥanbal, by Ibn al-Jawzī (2016)

Mission to the Volga, by Ibn Faḍlān (2017)

Accounts of China and India, by Abū Zayd al-Sīrāfī (2017)

Consorts of the Caliphs: Women and the Court of Baghdad, by Ibn al-Sāʿī (2017)

A Hundred and One Nights (2017)

Disagreements of the Jurists: A Manual of Islamic Legal Theory, by al-Qāḍī al-Nuʿmān (2017)

What ʿĪsā ibn Hishām Told Us, by Muḥammad al-Muwayliḥī (2018)

War Songs, by ʿAntarah ibn Shaddād (2018)

The Life and Times of Abū Tammām, by Abū Bakr Muḥammad ibn Yaḥyā al-Ṣūlī (2018)

The Sword of Ambition, by ʿUthmān ibn Ibrāhīm al-Nābulusī (2019)

Brains Confounded by the Ode of Abū Shādūf Expounded: Volume One, by Yūsuf al-Shirbīnī (2019)

Brains Confounded by the Ode of Abū Shādūf Expounded: Volume Two, by Yūsuf al-Shirbīnī and *Risible Rhymes*, by Muḥammad ibn Maḥfūẓ al-Sanhūrī (2019)

The Excellence of the Arabs, by Ibn Qutaybah (2019)

Light in the Heavens: Sayings of the Prophet Muḥammad, by al-Qāḍī al-Quḍāʿī (2019)

Scents and Flavors: A Syrian Cookbook (2020)

Arabian Satire: Poetry from 18th-Century Najd, by Ḥmēdān al-Shwēʿir (2020)

In Darfur: An Account of the Sultanate and Its People, by Muḥammad al-Tūnisī (2020)

Arabian Romantic: Poems on Bedouin Life and Love, by Ibn Sbayyil (2020)

The Philosopher Responds: An Intellectual Correspondence from the Tenth Century, by Abū Ḥayyān al-Tawḥīdī and Abū ʿAlī Miskawayh (2021)

Impostures, by al-Ḥarīrī (2021)

The Discourses: Reflections on History, Sufism, Theology, and Literature—Volume One, by al-Ḥasan al-Yūsī (2021)

The Yoga Sutras of Patañjali, by Abū Rayḥān al-Bīrūnī (2022)

The Book of Charlatans, by Jamāl al-Dīn ʿAbd al-Raḥīm al-Jawbarī (2022)